Masters of Modern Architecture

Other books by Edwin Hoag

The Roads of Man

American Houses

American Cities

Masters of
Modern Architecture

◆━━◆

Frank Lloyd Wright, Le Corbusier,
Mies van der Rohe and Walter Gropius

◆━━◆

by
Edwin and Joy Hoag

THE BOBBS-MERRILL COMPANY, INC.
Indianapolis/New York

Copyright © 1977 by Edwin and Joy Hoag

Published by the Bobbs-Merrill Company, Inc.
Indianapolis   New York

Designed by Gail Herzog Conwell
Manufactured in the United States of America

First printing

Library of Congress Cataloging in Publication Data
Hoag, Edwin.
    Masters of modern architecture.
    Bibliography: p.
    SUMMARY: Discusses the founding of modern architec-
ture through the lives and works of four important
architects.
      1.   Architecture, Modern—20th century—Juvenile
literature.   2.   Wright, Frank Lloyd, 1867-1959—
Juvenile literature.   3.   Le Corbusier-Galerie Heidi
Weber—Juvenile literature.   4.   Mies van der Rohe,
Ludwig, 1886-1969—Juvenile literature.   5.   Gropius,
Walter, 1883-1969—Juvenile literature.   6.   Architects—
Biography—Juvenile literature.   [1.   Wright, Frank Lloyd,
1867-1959.   2.   Le Corbusier-Galerie Heidi Weber.
3.   Mies van der Rohe, Ludwig, 1886-1969.   4.   Gropius,
Walter, 1883-1969.   5.   Architects]   I.   Hoag, Joy,
joint author.   II.   Title.
NA680.H54   720′.922   [B]   [920]   77-76888
ISBN 0-672-52338-8
ISBN 0-672-52365-5 pbk.

For

May, Clare, Gladys, and Elsie

Contents

WALTER GROPIUS — UNITY IN DIVERSITY

Foreword

Architecture mirrors society, from excitement to squalor; and as with all great human achievements, it is measured by individual acts. There is a non-illusory selfhood to a building. Rightly seen, it profiles the will, intellect, and creativity of its designer and the aspirations of its sponsor. *Masters of Modern Architecture* testifies to these truths, illustrating them dramatically while at the same time emphasizing the essential ingredient: the understanding client.

Architects are judged by their ideas. This is particularly true in a society such as ours, which is caught up in process, organization, bottom-line economics, and the quantitative judgment. Only those who possess an enormous quantity of ego-energy, such as the men described herein, can achieve the concentration of purpose necessary to escape into the realm of creativity and speculation.

In 1961 the Faculty of Architecture at Columbia University recognized these truths and the need for a critical reexamination of the central issues then facing society and architecture. They decided to hold a celebration to honor the "Four Great Makers of Modern Architecture," the same men presented here.

These strong-willed iconoclasts had decades earlier left what was safe and accepted and leaped toward visions of what might be. They were men who opposed the tide of public opinion in order to explore the edges of personal and architectural possibility. Following the progress of their lives and accomplishments is an exciting experience.

All were individualists, propagandists, and phrasemakers.

Each gave primary attention to the kinds of ideas that energize lives and free static attitudes. But each was different. Two were fractious and innate rebels with a genius for visualizing the opportunities of a special situation. One was primarily a teacher and theoretician who, as he became older, sought to escape personal limitations by advocating a team approach. Another was a perfectionist with unlimited patience and tenacity who carried structural simplicity to its new and sometimes boring essence. Each substantially altered the way we judge and use our physical environment. All are impossible to categorize because of the contradictory aspects of their personalities and works. All lived long and productive lives, buoyed by an inalienable personal ego and the belief that with their personal vision they could change the world.

It is impossible to imagine the twentieth century without these irascible men. Their ideas altered our buildings, our cities, and our way of life. Their presence is missed—the momentum of change they generated has decelerated.

The collective team has momentarily replaced the tenacious, soaring single mind. Quick-answer think-tanks and sullen computers collate convenient attitudes, and through mechanical media they resell the compromised results to the same unwary respondents. Architectural services are traded on the basis of the number of a firm's draftsmen. Initial cost is the gauge of excellence. The concepts these men gestated have been replaced by profit-and-loss statements. The epoch they animated is gone, but because of their life work, the seeds of continuing change are only dormant. Each of these titans left a legacy to future generations. Their lives document a battle between dull continuity and rousing change.

Their tribulations are related here with warmth and understanding. This book recaptures the excitement of Columbia's Four Great Makers celebration. It is possible that somewhere out there a young reader will recognize and accept the challenge.

Society needs the zestful vision of such a solitary new leader.

Charles R. Colbert, Architect-Planner
Former Dean of the Faculty of Architecture
Columbia University

Introduction

A new world has sprung up around us. We see it in our office buildings, schools, hospitals, airport terminals, banks, homes, and even churches. It's a world of steel and glass and concrete, soaring angles and curves, and elegantly handled space. It's the world of modern architecture: a child of our century, carried out in the building materials of our century, based on technologies of our century.

This new structural environment in which we live, learn, and work is the result of a cultural revolution that was, in essence, like any other revolution: it aimed at freeing man from the restraints of the past. Its chief weapons were technology and art and their successful merger.

We deal here with four men who led the battle for modern architecture. Largely unschooled in the formal sense, they struck out to change man's building in their individualistic ways, but with a common goal: to break away from the trend of their time, which was copying the temples of the Greeks, the castles of the medievals, or the shanties of the colonial fathers, and to mold a twentieth-century architecture for twentieth-century man.

Like all great men with revolutionary ideas, they were shot at and often hit—they were ridiculed and called mad or subversive by the powers-that-be, by the public, sometimes by their own profession. Like all great men, they persisted, firm in their conviction, and endured years of struggle before their points of view prevailed. And even today their work can set controversy simmering.

Many other brilliant, dedicated people helped our subjects

light their torches, and two generations of architects have since carried them. But Frank Lloyd Wright, Le Corbusier, Mies van der Rohe and Walter Gropius were the prime movers, the four horsemen of the modern movement. Hardly a building of consequence is raised today that doesn't owe a debt to one, if not several, of them. They were the masters, largely responsible for creating the vocabulary of modern building.

It is interesting that these four men, allies in a cultural conflict, were so strikingly different from one another.

Wright, oldest by a decade or so and a man with nearly as much arrogance as genius, was a lover of the land, dedicated to the harmony of structure and site. He brought the house down from its Victorian heights, stood firm with his Imperial Hotel during the 1923 Tokyo earthquake, astonished the world with his soaring Johnson Wax building, and created a controversy that still bubbles with his Guggenheim Museum in New York. Despite a hectic personal life, years of ridicule, and periods when he was flat broke and unable to get a commission, he was responsible for introducing numerous building innovations and for placing on our earth some of the most beautiful and significant structures extant. He will probably go down as the greatest architect in our country's history—just as he said he would.

Le Corbusier, a city slicker at heart, was for most of his career as uninterested in nature as Wright was intrigued by it. Instead, he envisioned man as defying nature, triumphing over it. Eccentric and generally grouchy, he was constantly involved in squabbles with the architectural establishment, government bureaucrats, and other factions of society. Also a painter and an incredibly prolific writer, he was continually turning out books, pamphlets, and miscellaneous tracts that proclaimed his views and attacked those who disagreed. "A house should be a machine to live in," he declared, and half a century ago he was building shining white concrete homes set atop columns, with ribbon windows rounding curves, and roof gardens. He played the shapes of cubism one against the other, molding concrete to his fancy. His Marseilles apartment block is a modern classic; his influence was admittedly the predominant one in the

United Nations complex; his city-planning studies have been models for students.

Mies, as conservative in manner as Wright was flamboyant, as frugal with words as Le Corbusier was verbose, was the precisionist, the most orderly builder of the lot. He dreamed of a new universal architecture, not his but man's. "I don't want to be interesting," he said in one of his few public utterances. "I want to be good." And about architecture: "Less is more." His Seagram building in New York has been called the ultimate skyscraper. His apartment buildings commanding Chicago's lake shore have been described as reflecting the very essence of architecture. Mies was the acknowledged master of skin and bones building—the strength of steel for the skeleton, the veil of glass.

Gropius startled the architectural world when he was still in his twenties with his Fagus factory, designed in 1911, half a century ahead of its time. It has been called the first truly modern factory. But he is known as much for his profound influence on architectural education—his dedication to teaching future generations of architects—as for his own body of distinctive work. He strove for what he called supra-personal architecture, architecture dependent not on individual genius but on the collaboration of talents toward a greater end. In Germany he founded and led the Bauhaus, a school that revolutionized industrial design in the 1920s; he later extended his influence as dean of the Harvard School of Architecture. When he was in his late sixties, he organized a firm called, characteristically, The Architects Collaborative and carried out projects ranging from the strikingly gleaming United States embassy in Athens to the sprawling campus of the University of Baghdad, Iraq.

These are the men primarily responsible for the structural world that surrounds us today. Their influence covers the globe, but their accomplishments were especially significant to the United States. Although Le Corbusier never left his adopted France, Mies and Gropius joined Wright in this country in the 1930s, as Hitler was rising to power in their native Germany. Our country was their principal battleground.

Frank Lloyd Wright

Man Apart

Genesis

With his flowing white hair, his modified Stetson and his self-styled clothes, he looked like a dandy version of Buffalo Bill. He had the arrogance of a Patton, the profile and ego of a matinee idol, and the genius of a Michelangelo. He stood only five feet eight and a half inches tall, but he appeared to be a much taller man. There was an air of majesty about him.

Frank Lloyd Wright strode through American architecture like a Gulliver among Lilliputians. He left his mark on three generations of young architects and half a century of design and construction. There are buildings under construction at this very moment, and many more to come, that will bear his legacy, if not his name.

A Victorian according to the calendar (he was born four years after the end of the Civil War and turned twenty-one in 1890), he was one of the most outspoken critics of Victorian methods and styles. Yet he was curiously at odds with the twentieth century as well. Born in the country, he hated the city and chose largely to ignore it, while around him America urbanized. During his lifetime the percentage of its people dwelling in the cities changed from a minority to a majority.

Wright was literally born to his trade. He was determined to transform architecture into a new entity based on new principles—his. His life was one of breathtaking innovation and striking success, punctuated by periodic harsh criticism from those within as well as outside his own profession. Although his achievements would have set the head of any ordinary man reeling, he felt, until well into his late years, that he had never really succeeded at home, in the sense that his work had not received the understanding and recognition it deserved in his own country. And there was certainly something to this view: throughout his long career he was never commissioned to design a single federal or state building.

In 1953, when he was eighty-three, Wright was asked how he felt about the fact that the American press and many members of his profession had not always treated him kindly.

He replied: "I don't see why they should have treated me kindly. I was entirely contrary to everything they believed in, and if I was right, they were wrong. It was a question at one time, I suppose, of their survival or mine. It is still true that the greatest appreciation of what we have done comes from European countries and from the Orient rather than from our own country. It has always been the idea of our people that culture comes from abroad. And it did, so you can't blame them for thinking so. They didn't want to hear of its developing out here in the tall grass of the western prairies. That was not exciting. In fact, they rather resented hearing about it in that sense at all. So when it had gone abroad and Europeans came over here, they could sell it to the American people—the people would take it from them, when they didn't like to take it from me."

There was an edge of bitterness in Wright's response, voiced six years before his death. Many architectural scholars disagree with his view, pointing to the honors heaped upon Wright here at home. And he was honored many times—he received a total of eighteen medals from various countries. But the point is that he viewed himself as a man alone, against his time, his profession, even his people; a man striving for a new truth and beauty and achieving it despite what he perceived as overwhelming odds. In this he followed his ancestors, hymn-singing Welshmen who boasted of their family motto: *Truth against the world.* He seems to have taken on this solitary perspective very early in life.

Frank Lloyd Wright was born on June 8, 1869, in Richland Center, Wisconsin. His parents were anything but ordinary people. His father, William Russell Carey Wright, was a charming part-time preacher and part-time music master whose forebears in Hartford, Connecticut, claimed family links to the poets James Russell Lowell and Alice and Phoebe Carey. William was a middle-aged widower with three children when he wandered to Wisconsin where he met and married Anna Lloyd Jones, a schoolteacher seventeen years his junior and the daughter of a hardy Welsh family of teachers, preachers and farmers.

Anna, in contrast to her new husband, was a strong-willed and dominating personality. But, like William, who enjoyed nothing better than losing himself in the beautiful strains of Bach and Beethoven, she felt deep appreciation for the beautiful and the great. Even before Frank was born, Anna decided her son would be a great architect. Believing in prenatal impressions, as was the fashion of the day, she spent long hours concentrating on pictures of cathedrals and other monumental buildings during the nine months the infant Frank was developing within her. And in preparation for his birth, she hung woodcuts of English cathedrals on the nursery walls.

When Frank was a child, his father accepted the pastorate of a Baptist church in Weymouth, Massachusetts, and the family packed up and moved there. It was a respectable, if modest, way of life. It was during the years at Weymouth that Anna attended the 1876 Philadelphia Exposition, where she purchased the set of Froebel blocks that the architect would remember many years later as being so important to him in his childhood. The blocks, invented by Friedrich Froebel, who founded the kindergarten system, were designed to teach color and form to preschoolers. A set was composed of variously colored cylinders, spheres, cubes and other shapes cut from maple. The components fit together neatly in designs and combinations. Only the imagination of the user could limit the number of arrangements. Young Frank, although then far beyond kindergarten age, spent hours on end with the blocks, rejoicing in the possibilities they held.

The Wrights had been in Weymouth only a few years when William, a restless man who was easily bored, decided his violin meant more to him than his pulpit. They returned to Madison, Wisconsin, where William became master of his own school of music. It proved to be only a temporary cure for his restlessness. In 1884, when Frank was fifteen, his father—long disappointed, sad, and weary—decided he could bear family life no longer. He and Anna sat down and discussed it, apparently rather matter-of-factly, and they decided he should go. Which he did. William Wright picked up his fiddle and walked out. His wife and his children never saw him again.

But William Wright left his mark on his young son in more ways than one. There was the love of music, of poetry, and of other great literature which Frank carried throughout his life. And, perhaps more fundamental, there was the idea that a man owed something to himself and his dreams that outranked all other allegiances, including that to his family. It was a notion that was to reappear much later in Frank's own life.

Nevertheless, the departure of his father—at a time in our history when such behavior was considered especially scandalous, reflecting even on those left behind—was shocking to Frank. It meant, among other things, that Frank had to find some way to help his mother make ends meet at a time when he was ready to begin preparing himself for his long-chosen career in architecture.

As a teenager, Frank was handsome almost to the point of prettiness. His mother doted on him and probably pampered him. But he was far from effeminate and had no fear of hard work. He spent several summers on the rolling fields of his uncle James Lloyd Jones's farm about thirty miles from Madison. He earned his keep, doing all the chores a boy does on a farm, and doing them until his muscles ached, then hardened. It was an experience Frank later recalled as "working from tired to tired." But on the farm he developed far more than a well-muscled body. He developed a lifelong appreciation and love for the honesty and harmony of nature. This feeling for the value of working with the natural order of things would characterize his whole approach to architecture.

Madison, Wisconsin, was a small town in those days; there were no architects around. But Frank found a job as a general assistant to a local contractor named Allen Conover, who also taught at the state university's school of engineering in Madison. For nearly two years young Wright divided his time among supervising construction jobs for Conover, doing his own sketches and designs, and studying civil engineering at the university. It was the only formal higher education he ever had.

There were several books that strongly influenced Wright's developing theories on how man should build. In one of the many books he read from his father's library, he noted the thought that the Renaissance was a sunset that men had mislabeled a dawn. This was the seed for a conviction that was to grow stronger with the years—the idea that architecture based on the styles of history was wrong. In John Ruskin's *The Seven Lamps of Architecture,* Frank was exposed to the notion that art and architecture are natural expressions and, as such, are controlled by laws of integrity and morality. Therefore, a building could be honest or dishonest. This idea stuck with Wright.

Now these were not only rather advanced ideas to be running around in the mind of a teenager, they were rather radical. Remember, Wright was born as the so-called Greek Revival period in American architecture was coming to a close. This was a stretch of about thirty years when hardly a structure of consequence was raised in the country that didn't look something like a temple of ancient Greece. It was a fad that left in its wake banks, schools, houses, churches, and even cemetery tombs that boasted the columns, cornices, and other trappings of the ancient Greek temple. Hard on the heels of the Greek Revival period was the Victorian era, which again was a half century of imitation. This time the structures copied were centuries-old European mansions, cathedrals, castles, villas, and other leftovers from times past. Even middle-class houses in the United States took on the look: they were built high, with narrow windows, turrets, towers, porches, piazzas, balconies, stained-glass windows, and jigsaw carpentry of every description as decoration.

Is it any wonder that Frank Wright, the maturing teenager, questioned the value of what he saw around him—an architecture of imitation, which was perhaps even dishonest or immoral? Anxious to get on with the real learning of architecture, Frank decided to go to the big city—in his case, Chicago. He discussed it with his mother, who was dead set against it. She pleaded with him to wait until he had received his engineering degree, until he was older. Frank dropped the subject, but it preyed on his mind. One afternoon near the end of his second year as a part-time engineering student, he took several old books his father had left behind, and a mink collar his mother had sewn on his winter coat, and sold them. With seven dollars in his pocket and without a final word to his mother, he took a train to Chicago.

Frank had an ace up his sleeve when he set out for the big city, and, after a few days of living on coffee and donuts and being turned down at architectural offices, he played it. It so happened his uncle, the Reverend Jenkin Lloyd Jones, had recently commissioned Chicago architect Lyman Silsbee to design a new church for his congregation. Frank applied at Silsbee's office. Silsbee took a quick look at Frank's sketches, instructed his draftsman, "Hire him as a tracer, eight dollars a week," and walked away. That afternoon, in one of his early flamboyant gestures, Frank borrowed ten dollars from the draftsman and sent it to his mother—evidence of his quick success in Chicago.

The early association with Silsbee was a break for Frank. Although Silsbee was hardly a revolutionary in architecture, neither was he caught up in the neoclassical movement of the times. His designs were rather informal and somewhat restrained for that day, but he was not restrictive. Young Frank, then, was exposed to the wide range of possibilities that Silsbee chose from, rather than confined to any particular individual stylistic movement.

After a few months, Silsbee raised Frank's pay from eight dollars to twelve dollars. But the young tracer thought he ought to be getting fifteen dollars a week and told Silsbee so. The architect refused. Frank walked out and got a job in another architectural office. But he didn't like it there and returned to Silsbee. The man looked up, pleased to see the return of the young talent. "So you're back. I'll give you eighteen dollars a week." Frank agreed.

Chicago was a good place for a young architect-to-be in those days. It had been only nineteen years since the great fire had burned most of the city to the ground. There was a substantial amount of rebuilding still going on. The rise of midwestern industry had created a new class of wealthy in the city, and they were having palatial homes built for themselves. So there was a good bit of architectural activity.

One architect whose work and words caught young Wright's attention was Louis H. Sullivan, a man then in his thirties, who seemed to have fresh ideas about things and who spoke of a new "democratic" architecture. Intrigued by the man and his concept, Wright went to the firm Adler and Sullivan and applied for a job as a draftsman. Again there was a bargaining session, for Wright was as convinced of his own brilliance as he was that he wanted to work for Sullivan. ("Early in life," he often told others later, "I had to choose between honest arrogance and hypocritical humility. I chose honest arrogance and have never seen reason to change.") Wright emerged with twenty-five dollars a week—and wished he'd asked for forty. In 1887, less than a year after joining Silsbee, Frank left to take up his new post with Louis Sullivan, the only man he would ever refer to as master.

Shortly before Wright joined his office staff, Sullivan had won an important commission: to design a great opera house, the Chicago Auditorium. The new draftsman was put to work almost immediately on drawings for this project, a twelve-story building which was to include a concert hall and a hotel. It wasn't long before Wright's extraordinary talents became apparent to Sullivan, and a special master-disciple relationship began to develop between the two men.

This growing bond between Sullivan and Wright was apparent to the other draftsmen and designers in the office. Some resented it. The newcomer was, in their eyes, an ill-educated hick from the country—and an arrogant one at that. Wright, for his part, probably made it plain he had little regard for

them. Co-workers taunted him about being Sullivan's "pet."
Wright did his best to ignore them.

For nearly a year Wright labored on the auditorium project,
learning as he went and listening—sometimes for hours on
end—to the older man as he expounded on architecture. Sullivan talked about the use of natural forms, about the texture of
a building's materials, and especially about using ornamentation in a way that made it part of a structure and not something
added to a structure. It was talk of a new architecture, and
Wright was intrigued by it. The auditorium was a great success.
Although they would hardly have guessed it at the time, it
would represent the pinnacle of Sullivan's career.

In the meantime there were several changes in Wright's
personal life: his mother joined her young son in Chicago, and
Frank met pretty young Catherine Tobin at one of his uncle's
church social affairs. Romance blossomed. Parents on both
sides objected when Frank and Catherine announced their
intention to marry. Catherine's parents even sent her away for
three months, hoping this would cool the romance, but it
didn't. Frank wanted to marry Catherine, and marry her he did.

By this time, his abilities having been thoroughly demonstrated on several major projects, Wright had a private
office right next to Sullivan's. The young man was the architectural firm's prize possession. To show it, as a wedding present
they gave him a five-year contract and advanced him enough
money to build a house for his bride on a lot in suburban Oak
Park which already held a small cottage that would be ideal for
his mother. Personally and professionally things were going
well for Wright. The world, it seemed, was his oyster.

Although Adler and Sullivan, like most architectural firms,
was most interested in big, important projects, influential
clients frequently asked the firm to design private houses for
them. Such projects were turned over to Wright. As more of
this kind of business came in, it became part of Wright's arrangement with the firm that he would work on these designs at
home in his spare time. Wright didn't mind this, because it
meant more money. Although he was then, at twenty-three, the
highest-paid designer in any architectural office in Chicago,

Wright was always behind financially. He neither smoked nor drank, but he was a man who liked to be surrounded by beautiful things. He liked to wear expensive clothes and to dress his growing family in the same grand fashion. It was a characteristic that would follow Wright through life. Even at the peak of his career, when he was earning very high commissions, he overspent and usually overowed. (Once, in later years, when he was being dogged about a fifteen-hundred-dollar debt, he borrowed ten thousand dollars, paid off the creditor, and, that same afternoon, went on a shopping spree with one of his sons. They spent the remaining eighty-five hundred dollars, buying, among other things, two grand pianos.)

One of the house assignments that came Wright's way under his arrangement with Adler and Sullivan was for wealthy lumberman James Charnley. Architectural critics have cited this project as the one that first revealed Wright's independent genius. The Charnley house was constructed in 1891, at the very peak of the Victorian era. It was extremely modern in comparison to every other house that was going up in those days, although it would hardly seem so to us today. It was a three-story geometric block with plain rectangular windows and a flat roof. It was built of horizontal flat brick and had a balcony projecting over the front door. Inside, it had a simplicity rare at that time. The house reflected concepts of design that other architects hailed two and three decades later as new ideas.

After a while, commissions to design houses began coming to Wright directly rather than through the architectural firm that employed him. Glad to have the opportunity to take on the designs and to earn the money, Wright carried them out—sometimes under another name. It wasn't long before he had a small business of his own on the side. And it wasn't long before Sullivan learned of Wright's extracurricular activity. He went into a rage, accusing the younger man of breaking faith. Wright maintained that what he did on his own time was his own business. They argued furiously. In the heat of it, Wright threw down his pencil and stormed out, not to see Sullivan again for years. He was on his own now. It was 1893, and he was twenty-four.

Houses for the Prairie

The break with Sullivan made the young architect angry and resentful at first; later he felt guilty. But it was a blessing in disguise: it forced Wright into a first step toward independent professionalism—opening his own office.

Something that had taken place earlier that same year helped in subtle ways to prepare him for this move. The Chicago World's Columbian Exposition, popularly called the World's Fair, opened. Under the influence of conservative eastern architects, it proved a triumph for the traditional, classical styles Sullivan and his young assistant abhorred. In fact, the Wright-Sullivan contribution to the fair—the Transportation building—was the only deviation from this historical style at the whole exposition. Wright was to say many times in later years that he felt the classical revival at the 1893 Chicago exhibition set American architecture back for generations.

As the young architect viewed the imitations of Greek temples and domes at the fair, his spirit of rebellion grew. The philosophy of architecture that had been developing within him began to crystallize: America should have its own "democratic" style, developed naturally out of structure, material and function—in Wright's words, an "organic architecture." The snobbish, autocratic models being imported from Europe were dishonest, for they bore false fronts not at all related to function. America's buildings, Wright now firmly believed, should honestly express both their content and their intent. The dominant line of the French Beaux Arts school (which all the

12

copiers were following) was vertical—man at war with nature. America's down-to-earth architecture should stress the horizontal—man in love with nature. For, after all, asked Wright, weren't the very symbols of nature different in the two countries? In Europe, a crowded, formal type of urbanization reigned. But in America, there was the freedom of wide-open spaces and beautiful landscape.

It was also at the Chicago exhibition that Frank came into contact with Japanese architecture for the first time: a half-sized model of a traditional wooden Japanese temple. He was already a devotee of Japanese art prints. (His own architectural drawings done in the early years of the twentieth century are reminiscent of Japanese prints in their graphic technique.) But now he became intrigued as well by their buildings: their union of form and nature, the way only light or transparent sliding panels divided inner space from outer gardens, the emphasis on horizontal lines.

Noted architect-writer Peter Blake has said, "Indeed, it is highly unlikely that Wright's prairie house, built in the first decade of this century, would have looked even remotely as it did if Sullivan's young apprentice had not seen the Japanese exhibit at the much maligned fair of 1893."

For some reason, though, Wright would always stubbornly deny this Oriental influence on his craft. It helped shape his philosophy, he conceded, but not the execution of his buildings. In a mellow moment he did admit a debt to the East for his concept of "interior space" (considered Wright's greatest contribution to architecture).

"Although I did not know it at the time," he said, "it was all there in the *Book of Tea* by Okakura Kakuzo, a Japanese classic: The reality of a room was to be found in the space enclosed by the roof and walls, not in the roof and walls themselves."

Though already the father of two children and burdened with debts from his high standard of living, Wright was hardly pessimistic in 1893. The young architect had an impressive record under his belt: twenty of the twenty-five buildings he'd designed under Silsbee and Sullivan had been built, including seventeen houses, a remodeled hotel, a school, and a boathouse. Two of his homes—for Charnley and for another client, Allison Harlan—had attracted attention for their fresh, simple style, their verve and original talent.

But above all Wright had a strong, sustaining self-confidence and a clear idea of the direction in which he was heading. In fact, when a wealthy admirer offered to finance him and his family for a four-year period of study in Rome and France—an almost unheard of opportunity for someone so new to the field—he refused firmly. "No, thank you," he said politely. "I'm going on the same way I've started."

The way he'd chosen was startling. It was as far as one could get from the Queen Anne–type home the revivalists were putting up, but it was also very unlike the "international" style of most of the so-called modernists of the day. "Inorganic" and "lacking in individuality" were two of the more repeatable terms Wright used to attack the work of such contemporaries as Walter Gropius, Le Corbusier and Mies van der Rohe, whom he called "glassic architects." In opinions voiced in later years, he said the United Nations building was a "tombstone—a great slab in a great graveyard"; the Lever house, "a waste of space"; the Seagram building in New York, "a whiskey bottle on a card table." The steel-cage frame, he felt, "was nineteenth-century carpenter architecture already suffering from arthritis of the joints," while boxy modern houses were "coffins for the living."

Like the internationalists, however, Wright wanted to develop forms suited to modern living and to new structural methods and materials. "The machine should build the building," he said, "but it is not necessary for that reason to build as though the building, too, were a machine." So, unlike the early internationalists, throughout his career he was to retain earthy colors, rich textures, and a degree of ornamental detail. Back when he constructed his first house in Oak Park, he made up his mind to destroy the box. He thought of walls not as barriers but as screens. And he so perfectly commanded and so dynamically expressed the free, flowing space that resulted that he was catapulted into worldwide fame.

The kind of life newlyweds Frank and Catherine enjoyed in their first home in upper-middle-class Oak Park was a fitting background for this fame. It has been pointed out that, for one who always said he hated the city, Wright relished every metropolitan pleasure during this period. He joined the tennis club in fashionable, adjacent River Forest; patronized the theatre, concerts and museums; attended church services with his wife every Sunday; and dined at the best restaurants.

Wright frequently designed Catherine's clothes, but his own, conservative in cut, came from one of Chicago's smartest tailors. To compensate for this conservatism in dress, he wore his reddish-brown hair slightly longer than was the style. (When he was in his eighties, however, he blocked out any published pictures of a long-haired Wright he could get his hands on, claiming they made him look effeminate.) Occasionally he knotted his ties in odd and original arrangements.

Though he never touched liquor and drank only a little wine, the young architect was the life of many a party, organizing charades and games. Frequently the parties were the Wrights' own, for they held lavish teas, cotillions and clambakes. Guests were greeted with beautiful fresh-cut flowers; resplendent silver and silk; elegant Persian rugs, vases, and hangings.

Guests were also greeted on many an occasion by the six Wright children who joined the union in rapid succession—all handsome, healthy youngsters. Their father indulged them lavishly, giving them their own bikes and horses, beautiful clothes, and musical instruments. Their playroom, which sported a mural from *The Arabian Nights* over the fireplace, was filled with toys and games made by Wright himself.

The playroom was just one of the additions to the Oak Park house. Two years after opening his office in Chicago's Schiller building, the architect supplemented it with a home studio. Connected to the main house by a corridor through the roof of which grew a willow tree, the place became known far and wide as "the house with the tree growing through it." The idea would later be used in many homes he designed for others.

Financing these additions and the other luxuries Wright was never able to deny himself and family was a considerable burden. It seemed that tradesmen, creditors and the landlords of his successive Chicago city offices were always waiting for payment. Frequently—like the time a grocer called Wright's attention to an eight-hundred-and-fifty-dollar bill—he was amazed at the size of the debt and immediately took out a loan to pay it off. Of course, this only postponed the day of reckoning.

Fortunately, by either instinct or design, Wright had landed smack in the middle of the almost perfect neighborhood for finding clients. Oak Park was a community of upwardly mobile professionals, where houses were occupied almost as soon as they became available. Soon he had so many buildings in the area (eighteen by 1901 and twenty-nine by 1909) that Oak Park was virtually a display center for his architecture.

His first significant residential commission as an independent, however, was the mansion he built in Oak Park's neighboring suburb, River Forest, for the wealthy William H. Winslow. "I could hardly believe I really had a job," the architect later wrote, somewhat belying rumors that were already beginning to ascribe a monumental ego to the young Wright. "Difficult to believe the initiative I had taken was now a reality. But I soon enough found out that it was."

The Winslow house was a simply proportioned, two-story home (the first story of brick, the second of tile), topped by a pitched roof of terra-cotta tiles with a deep overhang all around. Viewers were impressed by the high quality of workmanship, the richness of texture, and the distinction and quiet taste of the facades.

But two much less apparent qualities, radical at that time, later led professionals to single out the Winslow house as the most complete and the most independent creative statement ever made by an architect. These were the handling of composition, which gave a horizontal appearance to the two-story house, and the handling of scale.

The constant surprises provided by the great variety of views, the changing of floor and ceiling levels, the greater play of related and open spaces—these elements were all destined to become increasingly important in Wright's work. In the sixty-five years following the completion of this extraordinary home, there was to be much expansion upon the basic scheme, but the germ for all Wright's great contributions to domestic American architecture was already evident. It has been said that this house was itself an announcement of Wright's capability to lead architecture to a new age.

Very apparent in the Winslow house was the architect's own personal belief in the close-knit traditional family, the sacredness of hearth and home (a fireplace and usually an inglenook appeared at the center of almost all his 1890 designs), and the importance of group and family activities over individual concerns. All these attitudes were to undergo dramatic changes later.

But one attitude which remained unaltered was Wright's almost religious love of nature. It inspired him and often became the theme of his buildings. For instance, he once designed an especially efficient column after studying the structure of a morning glory. His tower buildings, supported by a single structural support, were based on the form of a tree. And his homes, always in perfect harmony with the landscape, bore a strong resemblance to natural elements.

"The Winslow house had burst on the view of that provincial suburb like the Prima Vera in full bloom," Wright liked to recall later. "That house became an attraction far and near."

A succession of wealthy, liberal-minded clients followed, and from 1893 through 1901 Wright produced seventy-one designs, of which forty-nine were built. This averaged out to eight commissions and five and a half completions a year. Among these were three apartment projects in Chicago, a golf club for River Forest, and a few stables and boathouses. But most were residences in the greater Chicago area, in Wisconsin where many Chicagoans summered, and a few as far away as Buffalo, Los Angeles and Texas. Wright's fame was spreading.

Each work bore what the prestigious *Architectural Review* in 1900 called the "intense personality, originality and unquestionable genius" of its architect. His designs soon earned the title "dress reform houses," because they were as unorthodox as the garment Amelia Jenks Bloomer introduced about the same period. Only once did Wright give in to conformity. A strong-minded Oak Park lawyer, Nathan Moore, demanded a typical Tudor half-timber "so I won't have to go down back streets to my morning train to avoid being laughed at." The architect, thinking about his then urgent need for money, acquiesced. But not without adding, as a touch of defiance, a porch—the first to ever grace an English half-timber. And not without regretting, as he later wrote, "the one time in the course of a long career that I gave in to the fact that I had a family and they had a right to live—and their living was up to me."

In the post-Winslow houses Wright began to discard his early symmetry for a more free and lively composition. There were also overlapping folded roofs reminiscent of his early Froebelian exercises. Especially noticeable was the development of a remarkable sense of site (one of his most brilliant gifts) that made his buildings seem both to have grown out of the ground and to have always been there.

When the new century dawned, however, Wright had not advanced too radically beyond his Winslow work in domestic design, and his reputation was still primarily regional. The year 1901 changed all that. It was a year in which all his theories, half-formed notions, and guesses seemed to jell into a remarkable synthesis. The year ushered in not only a new episode in his life, but a completely new era in architecture.

Though he had lectured and written for publication before, the architect, barely thirty-four, suddenly seemed to speak with new authority. Particularly noteworthy was his March 1901 address at Jane Addams's Hull House on *The Art and Craft of the Machine* (since reprinted many times and translated into several languages). Wright, always inclined to lofty, often obscure rhetoric, charmed his audience on this chilly night. The listeners found his Welsh musical voice, handsome face, and princely carriage as captivating as what he said.

The next day the *Chicago Tribune* editorial writer praised the speech as the first good word an artist had had for the use of the machine as a creative tool. What Wright had predicted was that technology would greatly increase the leisure hours available to man, altering his life and just as radically altering the appearance of his buildings. New methods of construction, he said, would enable modules of various kinds and sizes to be manufactured in quantity and assembled at the building site. And this would change the very nature of the architectural profession.

It was a shocking prediction, and during the first decade of the twentieth century Wright proceeded to make it come true. With modern machinery he built what were probably his greatest houses—those now known as the prairie houses. These homes were of such extraordinary strength and spirit that the period is called Wright's Golden Age.

He had long been disturbed by the typical American dwellings he passed going to and from Oak Park and his Chicago offices. He accused the houses of lying about everything, of lacking any unity or sense of space. He called them "ugly boxes cut full of holes to admit light and air, stuck up and stuck on, and not seeming to belong to the flat Illinois plains at all."

As his repulsion grew, so did definite ideas about the "new" prairie houses he would introduce to the scene. They took shape in 1900, in the form of pencil drawings for the *Ladies' Home Journal* ("A Home in a Prairie Town" and "A Small House with Lots of Room in It"). In one fell swoop he lopped off attic, dormer, basement, and the usual cubical and cramped rooms. All his houses hugged the earth and boasted flat, low, sheltering roofs with great eaves. With typical arrogance, Wright scaled them all to his own height of five feet eight and a half inches. (He once said any man taller than he was a "weed.") Interior spaces were open to one another and to the outside. Room flowed into room. "Characteristic of the New World," wrote one critic, ". . . space, freedom to move about, and ever-expanding frontier."

Windows were often continuous ribbons of glass. Dramatic and ever-changing views were integral: a sudden, unexpected source of light around a corner; a surprising glimpse of landscape; a tall ceiling swiftly followed by a low one. At the heart of every prairie house was a broad fireplace—a real one, not just a mantel. One hearth would be more comforting, he felt, than numerous small chimneys "bristling up everywhere to hint at judgment." For the exterior, Wright usually chose off-white stucco and dark stained wood. Outside were long parapets with concealed earth pockets from which vines twined upwards to soften the edges of hard masonry. The homes seemed to dissolve into the landscape, for Wright set each gently down on the ground, stepping it down until base and lawn were one. His goal, both inside and out, was simplicity—organic simplicity.

Of course, many of his prairie houses were not built on the prairie at all, but on suburban Chicago sites—River Forest, Riverside, Oak Park. The first two—the B. Hardley Bradley home and the Warren Hilcox home—were both in Kankakee, Illinois. Another, the Ward Willet house, sprawled in the shape of a cross in Highland Park.

Perhaps the most famous, the Frederick Carleton Robie house, completed in 1909 in Chicago, embraced all the elements of the prairie style to perfection. These included such innovations as the carport, floor heating, picture windows and casements that opened out rather than in, cathedral ceilings, and concrete slab floors built directly on the earth rather than over basements.

There was no skimping in the Robie house. Besides fourteen thousand dollars for the lot and thirty-five thousand for the building proper, Robie allocated ten thousand dollars for furniture Wright would design or select. These were handsome prices seventy years ago. The architect made no secret of the fact that his houses became painful to him once clients brought in their own belongings; yet not all the pieces he crafted were successful, particularly his high-backed dining room chairs. He even admitted himself, "I have been black and blue in some spot, somewhere, about all my life from too intimate contact with my own early furniture."

The *Architectural Review* called the Robie house "one of the seven most notable residences ever built in America." Other authorities said it was the most influential house of its era. Most of the ideas that characterize our modern American home— ranch style, split-level or whatever—had their genesis in Wright's prairie house of this decade.

Architectural scholars and students abroad were especially attracted by the advances the Robie house project made in the direction of standardization. Standardized bricks, shingles and clapboards were common enough, but Wright applied the process to many other parts: glass panes, window frames, doors, steel beams, concrete sections, cement blocks, and all sorts of fixtures. By basing his designs on the formats machinery could best produce, he could apply his architectural philosophy to public as well as domestic buildings. For though Wright was the only great architect who preferred building homes (of the eight hundred designs executed during his seventy-two-year career, about six hundred were residences), he did not entirely neglect public and commercial buildings. Early in his career he designed a mile-high Chicago skyscraper that was to be, he said, "a sky-city more permanent than the Pyramids." It was so far ahead of its time that it never found financial backing. Bankers were appalled at the thought of executives in suites among airplane paths.

During Wright's Golden Age, three of his nonresidential buildings symbolized as masterful and radical an achievement as his prairie houses. These were the Larkin Soap building, the Oak Park Unity Temple, and the Hillside Home School.

The world-famous Larkin Soap building in Buffalo (demolished in 1950) was a spare, beautiful cliff of brick. It was one of the first buildings with metal-bound plate-glass doors and windows, uniform metal furniture, and air-conditioning. It featured a four-story central well where office workers sat in sight of executives looking down from tiers of surrounding balconies.

The Oak Park Unity Temple, with geometric ornaments and a giant "egg crate" skylight for a roof, was the first example of the use of poured concrete in a monumental public building.

The Hillside Home School was fashioned by Wright from local timber and fieldstone for his aunts Jane and Ellen Lloyd Wright. It nestled on a gently sloping site near peaceful rural Spring Green, Wisconsin.

With such public commissions pouring in along with his residential ones, the twenty-four hours in every day were barely enough time for the architect. He worked feverishly, ideas constantly churning in his mind and going down on paper almost in finished form. He was also writing and publishing short essays on his architectural style and philosophy. These were sometimes stimulating, but more often they were a confusing mishmash, so wordy that some concepts were completely buried.

A reviewer wrote, "Wright's prose style is nearly unbearable. . . . He is endlessly repetitive, often contradictory, full of grandiose promises. . . . He is consciously Messianic, out to recruit disciples and votaries." Essentially the same criticisms were to be leveled later at the books he authored: *Autobiography* (1932, revised in 1943), *An Organic Architecture* (1939), *The Future of Architecture* (1951), *The Natural House* (1954), *An American Architecture* (1955), and *A Testament* (1957).

Labor went on in the midst of domestic turmoil, for none of his six children were ever denied access to the studio drafting room. There was also added noise from the kindergarten Catherine had opened in the added-on playroom. Wright seemed to bear all this with a certain benignity, even though the yoke of fatherhood never did rest easily on his shoulders. "I seemed born without it," he confessed at one point, admitting that his buildings inspired more of a father-feeling than his offspring, whom he regarded as "comrades, play-fellows to be responsible for."

To all outward appearances, Wright's domestic situation was as successful as his professional one. But as the first decade of the twentieth century began to draw to a close, things changed. Although he was probably one of the best known architects in America, debts weighed him down. When he failed to get several important commissions he wanted and needed, he became seriously depressed. He later said of this period, "I was losing my grip on my work and even my interest in it. . . . It seemed to leave me up against a dead wall. I could see no way out. . . ."

His relationship with his wife had become just as impossible for him. With the years, they had grown further and further apart. He was a handsome, romantic figure of a man; it was perhaps inevitable that somewhere along the line he would be attracted to a client's wife and she to him. It happened. The woman was Mamah Cheney, wife of neighbor Edwin Cheney, for whom Wright had built a small house in 1904. In the small gossipy community of Oak Park, their love was no secret, for they were frequently spied riding in the roadster that owner Wright had redesigned.

When Catherine refused to grant Frank a divorce, the gossip spread worldwide. In the autumn of 1909, Wright in effect abandoned his practice, entrusting uncompleted designs to a hastily selected colleague. He took off for New York and then

Europe with Mamah Cheney. Like his father before him, Frank Lloyd Wright left the domesticity that was bearing heavily down upon him. His parting shot: "Marriage not mutual . . . is worse than any other form of slavery."

The Turbulent Years

The first European stop for Wright and Mamah was Berlin, where Wright consulted with publisher Ernst Wasmuth, who was preparing a publication about the architect's work. Italy was next, and for several months the two explored bookshops and art stores. By the time they returned to the United States in 1910, Wasmuth's edition of Wright's work had appeared in Berlin, paralleled by an exhibition of his designs throughout Europe. There, almost overnight, the architect had become the most famous and widely discussed of his day. But in America, newspapers reviled him for his desertion of his family and attacked his work.

Mamah Cheney was divorced from her husband in 1911, but Catherine steadfastly refused to give Frank his freedom. Wright's mother, still staunchly loyal to her son, stepped forward with a gift of two hundred acres of farm land she'd inherited near Spring Green, Wisconsin. There the architect began to build Taliesin (which in Welsh means shining brow). Wright's mother, his children, and his apprentices visited him often in this building which was his home, studio, and refuge.

After moving Mamah into Taliesin with him, Wright—with his characteristic flair for the dramatic—called a press conference to tell reporters about their relationship and to generally propound his unconventional ideas about such arrangements.

Dressed in an elegant crimson robe, he stood before the great Taliesin fireplace as he talked. Mamah, attired in a regal Oriental gown, sat nearby. The architect probably hoped to mend his broken relations with the journalists and the country at large by explaining his liberal views of morality, but he ended by scolding reporters for criticizing his actions.

Women, who had been Wright's most admiring clients, were scandalized by his behavior—shocking in those days—and were not at all influenced by his attempts to justify it. They stopped commissioning residences or urging their husbands to hire Wright. This was quite a blow to his bank account. He built only thirteen of thirty-one designs during his four years with Mamah. In 1912, 1913, and 1914 only six full-fledged buildings were executed for paying customers. With so little money coming in, the architect had to support two households. And there was the added expense of building Taliesin (a never-ending task, for it was constantly being added to, altered, or renovated).

One sizeable job that came along, apparently just in time to avert disaster, was a commission to design Midway Gardens on the South Side of Chicago. It was to be "the most beautiful and complete concert garden in the world." The contract came from young Edward Waller, son of the man who had once offered to finance Wright on a European study tour. The architect set to work immediately on the spectacular block-long Midway Gardens. He was assisted by his son John, who did an abstract mural for the bar.

Things seemed to be going better for him as the summer of 1914 began. Community disapproval faded somewhat into the background as Frank and Mamah lived discreetly on the fringes of community participation. And a successful exhibition of Wright's work at the Chicago Architectural Club was a boost to his morale if not to the number of commissions he received.

As it turned out, though, this was simply the calm before a storm of tragedy—tragedy for the world in the form of World War I, and tragedy for Wright personally. It was noontime, August 14, 1914, when the architect and his son sat down for a quick lunch in the Midway Gardens bar, which was in a part of the building that was already completed. They were interrupted by a telephone call from Madison announcing that Taliesin was ablaze. With only this information, Wright rushed back on the first train from Chicago. He found a scene of devastating horror. Julian Carleton, a Barbadian chef hired only shortly before, had gone berserk at Taliesin, setting fire to the house and killing with an ax those who tried to escape. Dead were Mamah and her two visiting children (by her first husband), three Taliesin employees, and a local craftsman's son. The murderer was found and jailed, but he killed himself before he could be brought to trial.

After burying Mamah himself in her own garden, Wright isolated himself in the only part of Taliesin not destroyed, the working quarters. By night, he tried to sleep on a cot in the studio; by day, he wandered in dark numbness and despair. Ugly publicity to the effect that this mad architect, this family-deserter and adulterer, this free-thinker had gotten only what he deserved brought hundreds of hate letters. He tied them up and burned them.

But there were some expressions of sympathy—one from a complete stranger, a sculptress named Miriam Noel. She turned up in Wright's office to offer her personal help, and eventually became his new love. A divorcee, she had been living in Paris, but had been forced by the war to return to America. She was the mother of two married daughters and a grown son, and was the victim of a nervous disorder caused by an ill-fated love affair similar to Wright's.

With unfailing energy and courage, Wright soon returned to his only salvation after the Taliesin massacre—work. While construction continued at Midway Gardens, the rebuilding of Taliesin (with wood cut and stone quarried nearby) was also underway. Within a few months, Wright and forty-three-year-old Miriam moved into the rebuilt residence. Again Wright couldn't resist an emotional statement to the world, hoping to justify this new love so soon after the death of his former one.

But it was apparently a half-hearted attempt this time. The architect had already assumed his "persecuted genius" stance. It was, as one biographer said, "the interpretation of his life as a continuous battle against overwhelming odds, as a struggle for principle despite social ostracism, professional ignorings, financial loss, ridicule and rejection."

In an article in the *Architectural Record* entitled "In the Cause of Architecture II," Wright strongly attacked the Chicago School, a group of prominent architects known collectively by that name. He claimed sole credit for practically every trend in architecture and broke sharply with all professional schools. As a result of such rhetoric and impassioned accusations, he was labeled an irascible egotist, unwilling to say anything good about his colleagues or their work. These charges were to follow him all his life.

Only nature, the freedom of the individual, and his own work were free from the haughty criticism of the architect. A man deeply in love with his country, his only heroes were Emerson, Whitman, Thoreau and Thomas Jefferson (whom he praised as a man of culture and an architect). A long-time acquaintance admitted he'd never heard Wright express admiration for any European builder except perhaps Christopher Wren, who had commanded the respect Frank felt was due to men of his profession. In America, the only man he ever praised was his old boss Louis Sullivan. Even Michelangelo (whom Wright was often likened to) was not above reproach. "All Michelangelo did," scoffed Frank, "was set the Parthenon on top of the Parthenon. You know about his dome for St. Peter's, don't you? He got the chain up to hold it just in time. Otherwise there would have been a disaster. Why, it's not a true dome at all."

Copiers and imitators particularly enraged Wright. These, in Wright's opinion, included just about every architect around, since he denied having any architectural antecedents. Everyone was, therefore, an uncomprehending plagiarist.

"Neither custom nor the habit of imitation exists in the world of the spirit," said the architect. "There man's faith in himself alone has credit." On another occasion, he remarked with a sigh, "If only honest seekers once mastered the inner principles, infinite variety would result and no one would have to copy anyone else."

It was mostly of plagiarism that Wright complained in the early 1900s. He felt that several commissions had been stolen from him while he was abroad with Miriam, that colleagues had slighted him and had failed to credit his influence or acknowledge their indebtedness to him as a pioneer architect. So he welcomed the chance to escape that came with an assignment that was to be one of the greatest challenges of his long career.

In 1915, royal leaders of Japan invited him to build the Imperial Hotel in Tokyo (the original had burned to the ground in an earthquake). Late in 1916, after a farewell banquet hosted by Chicago friends, he and Miriam sailed from Seattle to Tokyo, where he was to labor for much of the next six years. Though Miriam had loaned him several thousand dollars toward the rebuilding of Taliesin, he was close to bankruptcy at the time of their departure. The promise of a handsome fee for the Imperial Hotel job was the bright light at the end of a long, dark tunnel.

As it turned out, he earned every penny. First of all, the hotel site itself presented unusual problems: "Sixty feet of liquid mud overlaid by eight feet of filled soil . . . about the consistency of hard cheese" was how Wright described it. And the structure had to be guaranteed to be earthquake-proof.

The architect remembered the piers that support the Chicago railroad stations and office buildings in the sludgy soil that lies beneath the Loop. He devised a similar way to absorb the hotel's shocks. The central supports would be sunk into soft earth in order to hold up the floor slabs "as a waiter balances a tray upon his fingers." As he explained to his son John, who had joined him to help with the project, the building would roll with the punches, floating on a foundation of mud. There would be cantilevered floors with projecting beams or girders fixed at one end to a rigid support, and there would be many small parts to the building so that they could move independently of one another, giving protection against earth tremors. Everything would be fireproof except window frames and sashes, which would be too expensive in metal.

In addition to the monumental engineering problems, there were other difficulties. There was a language barrier between

Wright and the Japanese engineers and workmen who, for one thing, preferred working with their hands rather than machines. There was the rainy season, which interfered with construction. There was the zooming-cost problem, which led the board of directors of the hotel to threaten abandonment of the whole project. But Baron Okura, a staunch friend whom Wright admired, shamed the directors into continuing their support.

And, of course, there were domestic problems. Though Wright had an almost inexhaustible fund of energy, in Japan he found it increasingly tiring to work day and night and still cater to erratic Miriam. Her jealousy, her incessant chatter, her constant interruptions, and the way she kept her eyes riveted to Wright's face when they went out together—all were disturbing, to say the least. The architect found relief in reading, playing the piano, and taking trips around the country to buy Japanese prints for his noted collection. He also made a few trips back to the United States. On one of these, working out of a Los Angeles office, he designed the Hollyhock house (named after the flower motif in its ornamentation) for Aline Barnsdall; it was a "fantastic Mayan temple" rendered in exposed poured concrete.

Finally, the Eastern climate and excessive work and strain took their toll, and Wright became very ill. His mother, then eighty years old, crossed the Pacific to care for her son. She was honored with a garden party hosted by the emperor.

Despite the many setbacks, the Imperial Hotel rose upon its site outside the emperor's palace: an ornate, rich structure with an exterior of greenish-yellow lava and gold-colored brick, blended with copper. Infinite variety was provided by terraces and courts, big and little pools, connecting bridges, graduating levels, narrow passages suddenly opening out into wide spaces. Each guest room was completely unique—something almost unheard of in hotel design. Here, as in most of Wright's work, the element of surprise was very important.

Wright was so taken with the smallness of everything Japanese that he made some of the hotel balcony doors barely five feet high. And windows overlooking gardens and courts were so low that only midgets could enjoy the view. Yet, paradoxically, doorknobs on guest room doors were high— small Japanese maids could reach them only by stretching up on tiptoe.

The Japanese were just as taken with their visiting builder as he was with them. On the day of his final departure, it was reported, "Workmen of every rank from sweepers to foremen of 'the trades'—laughing, weeping, wanting awkwardly to shake hands—crowded around him, shouting 'Banzai, Wrieto-San, banzai!' "

The hotel was in full operation by July 1922. Just thirteen months later, on the street in Los Angeles, Wright listened in disbelief as newsboys cried out this headline: "Terrific earthquake wipes out Tokyo and Yokohama." Days of uncertainty and conflicting reports followed, but Wright refused to believe the Imperial Hotel had gone down. Then came a memorable cable from the Baron, later flashed around the world: "Hotel stands undamaged as monument of your genius. Hundreds of homeless provided by perfectly maintained service. Congratulations."

Even the reflecting pool Wright had insisted on keeping— despite spiraling costs—helped. It was the only water available, and boys formed a bucket brigade to put out the great wall of fire that came sweeping over the city in the wake of the disaster. (The hotel was torn down in 1967 despite worldwide protests and pleas for its preservation.)

Wright lingered for a while in Los Angeles. He designed several homes in California, using a new method he had developed—an inexpensive technique using reinforced concrete blocks in a closed, cubical style. The finest example was the 1923 La Minitura built for Mrs. Alice Millard in Pasadena.

But such projects seemed tame after the Imperial Hotel. Wright soon gave up his California practice, announcing that he found "building conditions in the southwest a shallow sea of cheap expedients."

Back at Taliesin, he received long-awaited news: his wife Catherine had finally agreed to a divorce. Wright married Miriam Noel in a dramatic midnight ceremony on a bridge over the Wisconsin River. He hoped the legal ceremony would bring calmness and stability to the highly excitable, emotionally unpredictable woman. But it only seemed to make her more restless and vindictive. Even several consultations with a highly respected psychiatrist in Chicago brought no relief. Miriam left Frank in April 1924, after only five months of marriage. From then on she conspired to make his life miserable by harassing him with legal suits, portraying him to reporters as an eccentric, immoral man, and even breaking into a home he'd rented and smashing several hundred dollars' worth of furniture.

His domestic difficulties again affected his work, this time practically bringing his practice to a standstill. From 1915 to 1932, Wright got only thirty-five commissions, an average of only two a year. And twenty-nine of these were won before 1924, the year of his legal wedding to Miriam; he acquired only five thereafter. World War I and Wright's frequent absences from the country were part of the problem, but it was mainly his marital difficulties and the hounding, scandalous publicity that made the 1920s a personal disaster for him even before the stock market crash. "I wanted fame," he told a friend near the end of his life. "I hungered for it. But instead I got notoriety."

The few designs he did execute during this period reflected his changed attitudes toward society, the family, and the home. There were no more prairie houses with their openness and communication with nature. Instead his residences were impregnable cubed fortresses, retreats from a hostile world, tightly organized and turned inward. Some said they resembled mausoleums more than homes. One, the Freeman house, was the scene for a horror movie starring Vincent Price.

Despite his dislike for the city (he said it was evil, a hangover from feudal times, and was destined to disappear), Wright designed a number of skyscrapers in the late 1920s. There was the thirty-two-story National Life Insurance building in Chicago (1924), a housing development called St. Mark's-in-the-Bowerie (1929), and the Gordon Strong Automobile Objective (1925). None of these was actually built, but later the drawings would be dusted off and used in the design of other structures.

In line with this move toward public structures, Wright

announced that on January 1, 1925, he would open an office in Chicago that would accommodate twelve draftsmen. The firm would devote itself exclusively to commercial building.

The new office didn't materialize, however, for misfortunes continued to accumulate. His mother and several other close relatives had died not long before. Then another fire, caused by defective telephone wiring, did many thousands of dollars of damage at Taliesin II. It also destroyed about twenty-five hundred dollars' worth of books, blueprints and architectural drawings. He was forced to sell his Oak Park home and auction off his hundred-thousand-dollar Japanese print collection (which brought only thirty-seven thousand dollars). The financial burdens of again rebuilding Taliesin (for Wright obstinately refused to let it die), of paying alimony to Miriam, and of paying salaries to apprentices left the architect penniless. Wright was forced to sell shares in himself, against his future earning power. Several friends came forward to form "Wright Incorporated." The organization was authorized to issue stock and to take control of his estate and finances.

The dark depression days of the 1930s saw many of Wright's projects die uncompleted: a three-hundred-room winter resort hotel in Arizona; a nineteen-story apartment house and office building in New York; a summer colony for Lake Tahoe, California; an enormous ranch complex for the Sierra Madre; a planetarium enclosed in a spiral automobile ramp for Sugar Loaf Mountain, Maryland; and an amazing steel cathedral with chapels for all denominations. The latter, which was to hold a million people, would have been the tallest building in the world. A particular loss to architecture was the Elizabeth Noble apartment house, described as a "small, horizontally oriented structure of glass and concrete with wood-sheathed, cantilevered balconies"—an entirely new, fresh rendering of a small apartment complex.

Those who saw these designs recognized that Wright's genius and creativity were far from depleted. But the loss of many impressive commissions, which would have brought him additional fame as well as substantial fees, convinced many that his practicing days were over. Also, the extensive lecturing and writing he did during this period led many to consign to him the role of elder statesman, a stature he relished, but not as associated with retirement. When the Museum of Modern Art staged its historic 1932 show of international-style architecture, Wright was represented. But, in effect, he was considered already dead and buried as a builder.

As could be expected, this only made the master more determined to show that he was still alive and kicking—mainly kicking. He deliberately fostered his reputation as a caustic critic—a crusader willing, even eager, to confront society. A showman and salesman (which our great architects are often forced to be), he was adept at stealing headlines. He formed the habit of walking unannounced into the office of anyone he wished to see. His readiness to insult everyone and everything, to pop off on issues he knew nothing about, and to bluntly denounce every trend in American art and life won him many a spot in newspapers and on radio. When invited as a guest on a panel show, he customarily refused to relinquish the mike or podium and did all the talking. With his eccentric getup and his flamboyant manner, he was certainly "good copy."

As one observer on the scene wrote, "In his assaults upon taste, Frank Lloyd Wright, the man of the magnificently delayed entrance, the blackthorn cane, the riverboat hat, the white suit, the black cape closed by a gold chain, was an arresting public accusation. He was an imperious showman whose words came gently from a desert face puckered and creased like an apple left on a February branch. His were seldom gentle words, though; they were cutting images of Welsh forensic."

Wright once wrote, "The originality of my work has never swerved from first to last." This made him impatient and reproachful of some of his young apprentices, who, in his words, "sold him out by going too easily with the current of commercial degeneration."

Their usual answer was, "But Mr. Wright, we have to live." To this Frank would reply, "Why? . . . I don't see why anyone 'has' to live—at any rate, not live as a parasite at the expense of the thing he loves."

He had a penchant for visiting cities and then denouncing their architecture. He called Milwaukee's new county building, the pride of citizens and government officials, a "pseudo-classic horror!"; the Radio City Music Hall in New York City, that "crime of crimes"; the Metropolitan Museum, a "Protestant barn"; and a university in the west, "a good place for a trainload of dynamite." An office building in California struck Wright as "a dish of tripe," and Los Angeles "was much worse than the average American city because there is so much more of it to be ugly."

Asked by an interviewer how he would improve Pittsburgh, he snapped, "Destroy it and start all over." In Chicago he said that the Michigan Avenue building of the respectable University Club was "an effete gray ghost with less vitality than a smokestack." In Houston, when friends drove him past the towering Shamrock Hotel, Wright remarked, "I can see the sham, but where's the rock?" New York was "a vast prison with glass fronts, incongruous mantrap of momentous dimension." For Washington he recommended, "Preserve it as a museum piece. Then we should build a new capital city, not historic but prophetic." And about Boston: "What this city needs is five hundred first-class funerals."

His insults were not limited to cities and architecture. He once told an audience of advertising men, "There's not enough integrity in the whole bunch of you to make one decent man"; and to a group of club women he said, "Those hats you are wearing are monstrosities; I can't understand why you don't throw them away." Author Ernest Hemingway, who had once questioned a Wrightian conception for the Grand Canal in Venice, was dismissed by Wright as nothing more than "a voice from the jungle." And an address by the prominent dean of the Massachusetts Institute of Technology was termed "an unctuous falsification of modern architecture."

Much of his reputation as the nation's scold may have been contrived by Wright himself with a twinkle in his eye. He evidently relished shocking people. But the myths and legends that sprang up about the architect soon began to almost obscure the individual and his genius. Many Americans were unable to separate his art from his notorious personality. Few had not heard about or read about his background of "unbridled sin," including marital and extramarital escapades, berserk servants, financial insolvencies, legal battles, and indentured apprentices.

All of this probably played a part in his being omitted from the planning committee of the 1933 Chicago World's Fair, a monumental slight. But there were other honors to make up for it: election to the Royal Academy of Fine Arts in Belgium, and five years later to similar institutions in Brazil and Berlin; an invitation to visit Rio de Janeiro as a guest of the Pan American union to judge competitive entries for a Christopher Columbus memorial (hordes of admiring students dogged his footsteps there); an exhibition of his work that toured the world in 1931; a first showing (finally) in New York City under the auspices of the Architectural League of America; and the winning of the Florentine Gold Medal, which, Wright liked to brag, even Dante coveted but didn't win.

But for the most part, in his own country Wright was mainly thought of as an irritable, outspoken old man. This image was strengthened when he got a broken nose in a street fight in Madison (his apprentices later found and whipped the adversary), and when he dramatically hired a bodyguard after receiving a kidnap threat from an organization that called itself the Vigilantes.

Because he'd built nothing significant in ten years, it became easy to dismiss Wright as a notorious "over the hill" eccentric. But, as he'd done so many times before, this uncommon man rose above staggering tragedies, personal misfortunes, and financial reverses to again astonish the world with a veritable flood of innovative ideas and buildings.

Achievement Anew

What put Wright back on his feet, beginning about 1936, was a series of commissions from men as highly individualistic as he was. But a good share of the credit must also go to the fourth important woman in his life. Olga Milanoff, a European divorcee, was the granddaughter of a Montenegrin general, the daughter of a judge, and the mother of a seven-year-old daughter Svetlana. Wright was immediately fascinated by Olga's dark, exotic beauty when he spied her sitting nearby at the Petrograd Ballet in November 1924. Miriam had stormed out of Taliesin a few months before, and Wright was never able to be without female companionship for long.

At once the fifty-seven-year-old architect began wooing the twenty-six-year-old beauty. He won her in a matter of weeks and moved her into Taliesin III. Before the year was out, she'd given birth to Wright's daughter, whom they named Iovanna. Because of Miriam's vengeful delays of the divorce, however, Frank and Olga were not able to marry until August 25, 1928. The intervening three years were filled with legal suits, accusations and threats, pursuit by authorities, even nights spent in jail—all instigated by Miriam. But in Olga, Wright seemed to have finally found a woman perfectly suited to his temperament—she was artistic, intelligent, and mystical, but at the same time she possessed a strength of mind and a will as imposing as his own. Friends often spoke of how happy he was with her, how she inspired him, and how tenderly she cared for him. With her arrival, Frank's turbulent period ended and a time of great fulfillment, both as artist and man, began.

When the architect decided to turn the idle, neglected buildings of the Hillside Home School (operated by his aunts so long ago) into a school for young apprentices, Olga encouraged him and helped send out the first circulars on the "Taliesin fellowship." It opened with twenty-three apprentices. Olga cooked (boiled turnips were standard fare when funds were low), cleaned, and did any work required to keep the place going.

And the students worked, too. For Wright never pictured himself as any ordinary instructor, nor did he believe architecture could be taught in the traditional way. He believed learning would come through experience with materials, forms, and colors. During spring and summer the young people worked outdoors on farm chores and gardening—in line with Wright's insistence that "architects must be strong in body and character." Happily they waited on table and even did the family laundry for the privilege of having a bench in the master's drafting room.

The head of Taliesin had a current of excitement within him that could be turned on like an electric charge and transmitted to his followers. He also had the ability to convince students that he was personally interested in each one's career. And he was, often keeping track of each young person long after he or she had left the school.

There was plenty of recreation interspersed with the work. On Sunday nights, the fellowship gathered in their best dress clothes for dinner and a discussion of every possible topic, from books to life. Distinguished visitors such as Carl Sandburg, Edna St. Vincent Millay, and Ring Lardner often joined them. Wright himself frequently lectured on the evils of urbanization, praising the vigor of cities but denouncing their ugliness and artificiality.

To make his urban theories tangible to apprentices, Wright put them to work on his concept of what cities should be—a scale model of Broadacre City. This was a self-contained community where the bulk of the population lived in individual homes, each of which stood on an acre of land, close to fields and flowers. This plan for a decentralized America was preached consistently by Wright after 1935, and the model eventually visited many cities. It anticipated by three decades many of the criticisms of urban centers voiced in the 1960s.

One of the few Wright settlements to actually evolve from Broadacre City was a group of low rectangular houses built as a cooperative venture in the late 1940s and 1950s near Galesburg, Michigan. His most successful planned community remained his own Taliesin fellowship, which spent its summers in Wisconsin and its winters at Taliesin West, which Wright and his students built in Paradise Valley near Phoenix, Arizona.

If you had suddenly come upon the Taliesin West buildings in the desert, their beauty would have taken your breath away. Their walls of desert concrete, their gold, green and quartz stones, gathered by apprentices and bound together by more concrete, seemed to meld into the cacti and the barren rock. Deeply cantilevered roof rafters were topped by colorful canvas. Surrounding the main buildings were student architects' tent houses, with waist-high rock walls and more canvas roofs.

Life at both Taliesins was much the same—strictly regulated by Wright, who issued orders about smoking, drinking, late hours, sloppy posture and untidy clothes. He was speaking the truth when he told a newspaper reporter that apprenticeship there was "much like it was in feudal times . . . ," and that the workers cooperated "like fingers on my hand." For example, the only holidays celebrated were Christmas, Thanksgiving, Easter, and Wright's birthday, when each student would present the master with an "art box" he himself had crafted.

But while Wright's apprentices curried his favor and lived in subservience to his authority, they also learned. For he put them to work on the construction sites of impressive new projects which, after 1936, catapulted the architect back to the top of his profession.

Wright's luck began to change when a young man named Edgar Kaufman, Jr., a member of the fellowship, persuaded his father, a Pittsburgh department store owner, to hire Wright as designer of a family weekend retreat at Bear Run, Pennsylvania. *Falling Water,* completed in 1938, was perhaps the most famous and dramatic of Wright's homes. When Kaufman Sr. took the architect to the rustic site where he wanted to build a country lodge, he showed him the stone boulder he and his wife often rested on there. As he often did, Wright immediately and almost mystically envisioned the structure he would build. The finished steel, concrete and glass house rested on that same rocky ledge; a trickle of water ran through it, and a tree rose upward through its roof. The house was cantilevered so daringly out over a waterfall that workmen refused to remove the scaffolding, fearing collapse. Wright himself did the job, for—as in the case of the Imperial Hotel—he never doubted his own work.

He also proved the soundness of his plans for his next notable project—the administrative building for S. C. Johnson & Son, makers of wax products in Racine, Wisconsin. Building license authorities challenged the strength of the twenty-four-foot concrete columns (resembling giant water lily pads with slender stems) used to support the roof of the main workroom. The architect always said construction codes were for fools, but he knew it was folly to defy them. So, while thousands of spectators watched behind police barricades, the showman Wright directed a crane which dropped ton after ton of scrap metal on the wide top of one slender shaft. The column didn't crumble until sixty tons had been piled on—a safety factor of almost ten to one, far above the four to one generally accepted in static construction.

In the first two days of the building's operation, thirty thousand people came to stare aghast at Wright's odd chairs, the round bird-cage elevator, and the advertising desk flanked at each end with poopdeck-like structures (earning it the name Santa Maria).

In 1947 he built the sixteen-story Johnson Wax Company Research Tower in Racine. In 1953 in Bartlesville, Oklahoma, he built the Price Tower, which was completely sheathed in glass tubing. Both were supported by central cores inserted deep in the ground, from which floors were cantilevered like branches from a tree. From the edges of the floors hung curtain walls. More and more modern buildings are now using this revolutionary plan.

Just as Wright's preference in the 1930s shifted from level sites to hillsides, ravines, and even piers to elevate residences off flat ground, so in the 1940s and 1950s he turned toward circles, spirals, triangles and hexagons. The house he planned for his son David in the Arizona desert was a spiral, and the one he designed for his son Robert Llewelyn near Bethesda, Maryland, was made of cantilevered segmented circles. The Greek Orthodox church in Wisconsin (which Wright bragged was more Byzantine than anything officials could have copied) was designed in the form of a double saucer.

Wright's remarkable Guggenheim Museum, which looms up so challengingly on upper Fifth Avenue in New York, overlooking Central Park, is a snail-shaped structure. Finally finished in 1959 after years of endless conferences, revisions and snarling red tape, it was the architect's first building in Manhattan. With this commission he opened an office in the Plaza Hotel which he maintained until his death. The Plaza was one of the few buildings he admired in the city.

What Wright did for the Guggenheim was twist a three-quarter-mile gallery into a spiral ramp with a three percent grade. After an elevator ride to the top, the viewer walks down the ramp, looking at the art. An overhead skylight dome and window slits under the ramp provide unusually abundant natural lighting.

"With complex engineering Wright offered a deceptively simple solution to problems that had plagued museums for years," said one critic. But others said that visitors feared for their balance on the ramps, and that the structure was more an architectural showplace than a fitting background for art, which it was supposed to be. There were also complaints of cramped offices and an echoing auditorium.

The Guggenheim was only one of many unusual buildings Wright designed during the 1940s and the 1950s, their daringness and range of ideas dwarfing many of his previous efforts: the Beth Shalom Synagogue, an inverted hexagonal fiberglass cone perched on top of a triangular, poured-concrete base to form an abstract Star of David; the triangular glass and fieldstone Unitarian Meeting House in Madison, Wisconsin, with crisscrossed light baffles above the rostrum; the windowless brick gift shop with the sweeping spiral staircase in San Francisco; the monolithic hexagonal Kalita Humphreys Theatre with the revolving stage in Dallas; the massive Marin County Civic Center north of San Francisco; and the gay, beautiful buildings for the Florida Southern College campus. The list goes on and on, including dozens of fantastic projects that never saw the light of day: a saucer-shaped resort hotel suspended from a mountaintop, a floating garden, and even a drive-in mortuary.

During his renaissance, Wright also experimented with prefabricated houses and showed what he could design for a moderate price—he called them "Usonian," from a coined word meaning the United States of North America. One he built near

Madison for Herbert Jacobs became a kind of pilot project for simple and dignified low-cost residences (fifty-five hundred dollars, including architect's fee). Some even achieved an appearance of elegance. The concept had great appeal, despite a few minor idiosyncrasies of the architect, such as a dislike for closets. Many were eventually built all over the country. Wright described the Usonian as "a thing loving the ground with the new sense of space, light and freedom."

As he advanced toward the end of his long life, his arrogance diminished not one bit. Once when he and Olga were visiting old and close friends in Chicago, the host couple were away until evening. Wright said to his wife, "Let's rearrange their living room for them. It really needs improvement." Though doubtful how this gesture would be received by the hosts, Olga went along. All day the two pushed and pulled furniture, including a heavy grand piano. They even journeyed to a florist to bring back armfuls of foliage to add greenery to the room.

Needless to say, the couple didn't appreciate their changed living room and maintained a stormy silence all through dinner. The next morning when the Wrights arose, they found the room restored to the original state. Even the foliage had disappeared. "What a shame," Frank said to the embarrassed Olga. "We had made it so beautiful for them."

His writings became closer and closer to pure self-adulation. Twice in one book he placed himself third man on the totem pole: Lao-tse, Christ, then Wright. When fans flatteringly told him he was the world's greatest living architect, he asked, in all seriousness, "But who else is there?"

His tongue became more and more barbed. The most pungent attacks were reserved for members of his own profession and their products. International-style buildings he labeled boxes. Steadfastly refusing to join the American Institute of Architects, he called its eminent members "old men afraid to go out without their rubbers." (They gave him their Gold Medal, but later awarded another their 1957 Centennial Medal as Architect of the Century.) Upon meeting noted architect Phil Johnson soon after he and Mies van der Rohe had completed their famous Seagram building in New York, Wright asked,

"Are you two still putting up little buildings and leaving them out in the rain?"

He would brook no criticism of his work. When some books didn't fit on shelves of a library he'd designed, he said, "Let them buy books that do fit, then." When pictures were too tall for his museum walls, he commanded, "Cut them in half," brandishing his cane. When one of his roofs leaked into a guest's bowl of soup, he advised the lady to move over. When he designed a mile-high needle-shaped tower for Chicago's lake front to accommodate a hundred and fifty thousand employees, someone pointed out that the whole center of Chicago would have to be razed to move people, supplies, and services in order for it to be built. Wright simply said, "Well, so be it." And when tenants of one of his hexagonal houses rebelled against a bathtub in a shape to match, the architect warned, "If you start compromising now, I quit."

He was more and more excused for such impudence, though. So commanding was the presence of this noble figure with the handsome face that most people almost involuntarily rose to their feet when he entered a room.

Wright was also excused many times for structural defects. Sometimes a client who had knocked his head against doors and trellises Wright had arbitrarily designed to his own height would compile a list of leaky roofs, parting seams, cracking walls, and tortuous corridors. But more often he would be won over by the sheer beauty of the place.

Robert Woods Kennedy, a young architectural apprentice of Gropius, spent one of his vacations visiting Wright structures at Taliesin. "The trip threw me," he confessed. "On the one hand his houses were structural disasters: an endless series of sagging cantilevers; inoperable windows and doors; leaky roofs, windows and walls; cracked brick work and cracked slabs; peeling plaster. Not atypical for a pair of doors to have a nail in each, tied together with a piece of string.

"On the other hand," Kennedy continued, "they enthralled me. They were full of unseen beauties, marvelous effects, terrific manipulations of light and scale, and were uniformly splendidly sited."

For such virtues clients ignored the sins and flocked to Wright's office once again in his last decades of life. Often they docilely took dictation from the master about how they were to live in his buildings.

A typical client was Arch Oboler, Hollywood author, producer and director, who had grown up on the South Side of Chicago near an admirable early house of Wright's. Married and ready to commission his own first home, Oboler wrote the architect about taking the job. He was fully aware of the builder's reputation as a character "who strode through his world with rapier tongue and flailing Malaccan cane, striking down conventionalism, hesitant clients and architectural committees with impatient gusto."

One day, there was Wright on Arch's doorstep, firing rapid questions about his finances ("You know, of course, the banks won't advance you one dime on my designs"); about the quality of his work ("Do you write good things? I build good houses!"); about the site ("I suppose you'll want to build in that Beverly Hills. Cardboard crackerboxes covered with pink stucco").

Finally, after they agreed on a site (in the Santa Monica mountains, not in Beverly Hills) and on a price (twice as much as Oboler had wanted to pay), work began. On Wright's advice, Oboler and his wife left town on a vacation. Otherwise, the architect had told them, they would be changing the blueprints umpteen times and increasing expenses.

Wright then proceeded to do this very thing himself. He redesigned the whole front of the house on the spot, telling the contractor to "rip it out." And he would have substituted pine after four thousand dollars' worth of the originally proposed redwood had already been purchased, but the client put his foot down.

One day the couple was happily entertaining friends at a barbecue in their almost-completed Wright home when they spotted a caravan of low-slung imported cars winding its way up their mountain. From the lead auto majestically stepped the master himself; twenty of his disciples then alighted from the others. While the clients looked on helplessly, Wright ordered the twenty to "rip out" the redwood fence that had just been built next to the house. They did, then and there. "Now, dear friend," said Wright to Arch, "doesn't that look better?" Wright then doffed his cape and grandly invited his twenty followers to join his clients' barbeque.

As Wright neared his ninetieth birthday, he had never been busier or more active. There were more projects on his drawing board that eighty-ninth year than in any other in his entire career. Among them, still in sketch form, was a simple open pavilion whose columns supported a flat roof with sheltering, overhanging eaves. Showing the drawing to a visiting journalist, the architect said with some embarrassment, "I guess you can call this taking architecture all the way. This is where I will be buried, in the crypt beneath the black marble floor—very simple, very beautiful.

"But if I can just stay above ground for, well, three more years," he added, "we can bring in three million dollars in fees. There has never been so much work. Right now we have contracts for over eighty buildings, counting churches and houses."

As dapper a dresser as ever, the octogenarian still enjoyed racing around the desert in his favorite custom-built sports car. "Faster," he would shout at his driver periodically. And until the end he maintained the same busy schedule, writing in the morning and designing in the afternoon. He always worked in his Taliesin drafting room, sitting on his sheepskin-covered bench.

"A man slows down with age," he confessed. "It's inevitable. But I find it no drawback. I can do double—no, ten times—the work I once could. Now I just shake the answers out of my sleeve. . . . Every building is an experiment, but in the same direction. That's why I have to keep going. I can't rest. I never could."

On Easter Sunday 1959, Wright put all his work aside to join in the holiday festivities at Taliesin. The sixty-five apprentices scoured the desert for decorative foliage. The master's daughter Colleen arrived, as well as his sons Lloyd and David and their families. Other guests came from Phoenix and Scottsdale. The head of the fellowship made his usual grand entrance, in white from head to toe, a jet-black cape over his shoulders. During supper he regaled those around the tables with funny tales about the many legends generated about him and his work. With Olga by his side, Wright listened to the fellowship choir, watched the children hunt for Easter eggs, and viewed a movie on the life of Christ.

A few days later he was stricken with pain while at his drawing board. He was rushed to St. Joseph's hospital in Phoenix, where he underwent a successful, simple operation. But three days later he died. It was almost two months to the day from his ninetieth birthday. Only a few weeks before, he'd been heard to say, a little wearily, to a student, "Death is a great friend."

This country boy at heart was buried in the rural Wisconsin land where he was born and which he had always loved. His body was borne to its resting place by a horse-drawn grain wagon. The old-fashioned simplicity of the parting was most fitting. Later, after the pavilion he'd designed was completed, Wright's body was moved there.

Once asked by a client how he had endured such long years of hardship and tragedy, he replied, "At first people discover you, and everything you do is wondrous. Then they begin to look for feet of clay, and everything you do is berated. But if you live long enough, you become an old master. Now I am an old master."

But as a writer said in the *New Yorker* magazine, Wright was one of those few people who always seem to conquer age. He remained ever young at heart, eager and energetic, which is perhaps why young people found him so endearing. He could not go on without looking for new answers, and even in his ninth decade his fund of innovative designs seemed inexhaustible. On his drawing board when he died were a helicopter shaped like a top, an auto shaped like a paddlewheel steamer, a gas station with pumps hung from the ceiling so cars could be serviced from overhead, and an airborne chapel with a ramp and a parking lot below. With a twinkling look in his eye he'd always tap his forehead and say, "Plenty more up in the attic— plenty more." And when asked what he considered his greatest building, he'd reply, "The next one; always the next one."

By his own count he had completed more than eight hundred "next ones" before his death. He'd left the world a contribution that can never be equaled: innovations including foam-rubber seats, the carport (which he also named), indirect lighting, radiant heat, ribbon windows, the split-level living room, hollow-stemmed piers, plywood panels, built-in furniture, the simplified form, and the harmonious blending of home and setting. But even more important is his legacy of originality, individuality and integrity. His example was one of victory over every obstacle, and courage in the face of every adversity. It was impossible for him to compromise; he would destroy months of work at the drawing board, waive badly needed fees, and turn his back on entire projects if the work did not meet his standards of "good" and "true."

Some of the last advice he gave to a young admirer was, "The thing to do, young man, is play it straight. Every time I have had to compromise, it has grown like a great cloud of accusation against me. Always play it straight."

In his ninety years the architect did exactly what he had set out to do. His one ambition, he always said, was to see America get the culture and architecture it deserved. By the time of his death, he had led this nation out of architectural bondage and onto its own path of original beauty.

Eero Saarinen, a noted architect in his own right, said, "If this were an age like the Renaissance, Frank Lloyd Wright would have been honored as the Michelangelo of the twentieth century." To which Wright would probably have snapped back, "Michelangelo. Who's he?"

Le Corbusier

Poet in Concrete

An Early Course

On a windswept coastal landscape just a few minutes from downtown Marseilles, a startling rectangle of a building reaches toward the Alps on massive legs of concrete. Though newer, taller buildings now surround it, the structure continues to dominate by virtue of its sheer power and boldness and its ruthless simplicity. It is the Unité d'Habitation, the revolutionary apartment building which shocked and outraged many when it was finished in 1952. Even today, twenty-five years later, the tempest of controversy still simmers.

It is certainly like no other apartment building anywhere in the world. Into the huge slab structure were slid, like drawers into a bureau, some three hundred fifty apartments to house sixteen thousand people—all under one roof. Halfway up, a shopping center, post office, hotel, café, and other service facilities gird the building like a belt. Its roof garden supports not trees and shrubs but sculptural concrete objects, a wading pool, an open-air theatre, a nursery, and a cinder track. Fronting each apartment is a heavy balcony whose brightly painted sides extend like fins, causing the building to shimmer like a mosaic and creating a weird three-dimensional effect.

Citizens called the Unité the "nuthouse" or "the madman's house." A suit was brought against its architect for disfiguring the French landscape, and a group called the Society for the Preservation of the Beauties of France tried to have him forcibly restrained from despoiling the nation. City authorities re-

49

fused to run a bus line out to it, keeping it partly empty for years. The leading hardware store of Marseilles wouldn't furnish locks for the structure for fear of ruining its reputation. And prominent French psychiatrists warned it would contribute to the outbreak of mental diseases.

The man responsible for this monolith on stilts was Swiss-born architect Charles-Edouard Jeanneret, who early in life adopted France as his country and Le Corbusier (shortened to Corbu by admirers) as his nickname.

His buildings ranged from a small one-room vacation cabin on the Riviera to an entire city in India; from a tramp ship that's still sailing to a giant ministry in Rio de Janeiro, Brazil. Some of his structures were delicate, thin and light; others were heavy, broad and brooding. But all possessed the passion of a poet. Le Corbusier was the "poet in concrete."

He was a tall man, stern and stolid, with an egg-shaped head, a deeply carved face, and the lithe, wiry frame of an athlete. His blue eyes were always framed by a pair of thick, dark-framed glasses.

Arrogant, suspicious, and sarcastic, with an extraordinary knack for making enemies, the artistic genius nevertheless became one of the most renowned and influential architects of the twentieth century. Today his Marseilles block is one of the foremost tourist attractions in France, and signs pointing to it say "Le Corbusier Habitation."

Blessed with amazing stamina and a creative mind bubbling over with ideas, Le Corbusier produced, before his death in 1965, about fifty-seven buildings, more than fifty books, countless articles, pamphlets and manifestos, and an amazing fourteen hundred sets of plans. Always sketching, even in a plane or on a train, he filled countless pads with drawings of objects, sites, and structures that impressed and inspired him. These could be anything from the mighty Parthenon to a simple crab shell.

The painter and architect was also a sculptor, a designer of tapestries, and, secretly, a poet. Before anyone else had realized that a city could and should be planned, Le Corbusier was engaged in total environmental design. It is largely within his image of the city that most urban planners have functioned for the past forty years. With the eye of a prophet, he foresaw all the problems plaguing us now—traffic congestion, urban sprawl, slums—and tackled them head-on. But he never designed in a vacuum. The people who were going to live in his dwellings were his main concern, before aesthetics and form. He was undeniably Europe's finest symbol of urban humanism.

Le Corbusier was nothing if not a creator, an innovator. He was a born questioner, forever asking why, forever looking upon the world with a spontaneity and freshness. It showed in his work. Every project he left behind, even if only on paper, revealed some radical notion, some imaginative handling of a difficult site, or some significant design work. A reporter, after being guided through one of his structures by the architect himself, wrote that Corbu "had the dedicated air of a man deliberately staking everything on his theories."

This daring was an element in all his work, even from the beginning. Speaking of the very first house he designed at the tender age of eighteen for his Swiss teacher, Le Corbusier said, "Already I have risked a foolhardiness in defiance of the wise: two-angle windows." One of his earliest city plans boldly called for razing the center of Paris and rebuilding it from scratch. When others were still copying from ages past, layering their buildings with "doilies" and other ornamentation, he was putting up completely bare, starkly white villas on stilts in suburban Paris.

But, like his American counterpart Frank Lloyd Wright, Le Corbusier paid the price of being first so many times. Because he was so far ahead of his profession, his novel designs and buildings usually aroused outrage and derision. He was constantly embroiled in battles with authorities, politicians, and the press. "I'm like a lightning conductor," he explained. "I attract storms." Scorned and ridiculed by architects, journalists, and historians alike, his creative genius constantly eroded by others' pomposity and jealousy, Corbu soon developed what one biographer called "the disposition of a bleeding bull." Embittered, he was difficult to know and difficult to work with.

Oddly enough, the architect seemed to have a premonition of

his future struggles. When he was only twenty-one and had barely begun to build, he wrote his teacher a letter that contained this extraordinarily prophetic passage: "I have forty years in front of me to reach what I picture to be great on my horizon, which is still flat at the moment. . . . I want to fight with truth itself. It will surely torment me. But I am not looking for quietude, or recognition from the world. I will live in sincerity, happy to undergo abuse."

Charles-Edouard Jeanneret was born on October 5, 1887, in the Swiss watchmaking city of La Chaux-de-Fonds. He grew up hearing stories of how his ancestors, the Albigensians—a persecuted sect of French Huguenots—had fled there in the sixteenth century to establish the industry. There was always pride in his voice when he spoke of one revolutionary grandparent who died in prison, and of another who was among the leaders of the successful La Chaux revolution of 1848.

A studious boy who even then suffered from poor eyesight, he was a menace on skis. His mother, who lived to be one hundred, trained her eldest son to be a musician and informed her youngest, Charles-Edouard, "You will be a genius." He believed her.

Stamina, energy, and craftsmanship were characteristic of the Jeanneret family. Charles often accompanied his father, a watch engraver and an ardent mountain climber, on Sunday walks through the Alpine terrain. Here we find the roots of his interest in sports and physical fitness, and of his belief in the Greek and Renaissance notion of the "whole" man requiring a sound mind in a sound body. Sports equipped a person for the battles of life, he thought, so tennis courts, football fields, and stadiums were a part of all his city plans. The rooftop garden of his Marseilles block contains a thousand-foot cinder track upon which Le Corbusier posed proudly for photographers in a gym shirt and shorts and professional-looking sneakers. Even when he was in his sixties, he jogged before breakfast every day. And when he was in his seventies, he was still swimming daily.

On the Sunday walks with his father, the boy sketched— analytical drawings of fir trees and flowers, and more lyrical drawings of natural forms as ornamentation. His talent and interest in sketching were so apparent that at fourteen he was enrolled in the art school of La Chaux-de-Fonds, which had been founded in the nineteenth century as a training school for watch engravers.

Jeanneret might have remained a watch engraver had it not been for L'Eplattenier, a "delightful" teacher at the art school. He told young Charles, "You will be an architect," and he introduced him to the masterpieces of the past, and to the fundamentals of art.

It was L'Eplattenier who secured for Jeanneret, who was only eighteen, his first building commission. The result was the Villa Fallet, completed in 1906, on the shore of Jura north of his native town. But it must not have pleased the young architect, for he never mentioned it or included pictures of it in his collections. What is interesting is the careful decorative detail the young man was already using to translate nature into a strict geometric language.

With the fee from his first commission, Jeanneret left home to see and to learn. He went to Italy, where he admired the white stucco structures of the Mediterranean; to Vienna, where he learned the philosophy of Adolf Loos equating ornamentation with crime, and where he put in a brief stint in architect Josef Hoffman's workshop; and to Lyons, where he met utopian socialist Tony Garnier, who was already designing a prototype of the industrial city.

He ended his first journey in Paris at the age of twenty-one. He spent fifteen months there working for a progressive architect, Auguste Perret, who believed "decoration always hides an error in construction." Perret had already built the first tall, exposed reinforced-concrete frame building six months earlier. In a year and three months he successfully converted his young apprentice from Art Nouveau and showed him all the exciting possibilities of reinforced concrete: a free facade and interior plan, gardens on the roof, stilts or "pilotis" holding up a tall building and liberating the space beneath it, a tree principle of construction (the bottom recessed, and top floors cantilevered or projected out beyond) instead of the pyramid type typical of massive stone buildings, and the beauty and honesty of a brutally exposed concrete surface.

When Charles-Edouard had learned all this, it was time to

move on, this time to Germany to study advanced arts and crafts on a special scholarship from his former academy. The natural spot for him to settle in at this point in his development was a studio in Berlin—the only center then producing much advanced work and thinking in the field that was later to be called industrial design. Five months there seemed to speed by under Peter Behrens, chief architect for the A.E.G., a German electric utility company. Behrens had designed the company's notable steel and glass turbine factory, its lighting system equipment, its stationery, and a line of industrial products to produce what today we'd call a "corporate identity."

Coincidentally, two other young apprentices working at Behrens's studio at the same time were to emerge as outstanding leaders of modern architecture: twenty-four-year-old Ludwig Mies van der Rohe and twenty-seven-year-old Walter Gropius. All three had been drawn there because utilitarian building seemed the only channel for their particular energies and convictions.

By the time Le Corbusier left the German studio late in 1910, however, he had largely rejected the kind of functionalism Behrens preached. (This was to be a pattern throughout his career—first imitation and practice, then rejection as he progressed and developed.) The clean, orderly, precise, and puritanical Swiss part of him admired the technology of Behrens and his followers, but the romantic, imaginative Latin part of him insisted that art and beauty were separate from usefulness and efficiency. Too many "fundamentalists" were willing to put up ugly structures so long as they were less expensive to build and more efficient to operate, Corbu felt.

Later, when he was labeled a "functionalist," he would deny it: "This frightful word was born under other skies than those I have always loved—those where the sun reigns supreme."

In May 1911, at the age of twenty-four, he and a young Swiss friend, Auguste Klipstein, set off with knapsacks on their backs, to view those skies. With a new maturity capable of fuller understanding, he visited the older, classical Europe which he'd hardly seen in his previous travels. For more than a year he wandered through the Balkans, the Greek Islands, Asia Minor, and Italy, filling a pocket-sized sketch book with drawings, ideas, and impressions that were to inspire him in the years to come.

Le Corbusier was now ripe for a mistrust of academic authority, for he had seen the disastrous influence the Ecole des Beaux Arts was exerting on architecture not only in France but in other countries as well. It made building static and imitative, and it made education in the profession little more than an academic ritual where "correctness" was all-essential and the drawing of the structure more important than the actual building itself. It resulted in all the Renaissance windows, Gothic gables, Roman and Egyptian columns, and Grecian cornices that were cluttering up buildings in Corbu's day. And it strangled any attempt of new architects to respond to new ways of life and new building materials by labeling such innovativeness and creativity "heretical" and "blasphemous." When one visiting lecturer to the Ecole began to talk about building with concrete, he was hissed and booed and finally silenced with the students' cry that "we're not engineers."

Perhaps it was the thought that he could improve the teaching of architecture, at least on a small scale, that led to a decision Le Corbusier made in 1911, while still in Athens. There he received a letter from his teacher L'Eplattenier inviting him back to La Chaux-de-Fonds to head the architectural branch of a "new section" that the art school was launching. But before long Le Corbusier and L'Eplattenier had a falling out, the first of many such estrangements to erupt along Corbu's path.

The battle was characteristic of the bitterness, harping, and recrimination that became a part of the young architect's life during his next five years in the Swiss town. Corbu soon developed the biting, insulting, "chip on the shoulder" style of defense that was to become characteristic. Most of the designs and buildings he produced in his hometown between 1912 and 1917 might have won grudging acceptance by his self-appointed critics, but then came an exotic, screaming yellow "Turkish villa." Municipal authorities protested that it didn't go with its site. Corbu snapped back, "It is the setting that does not go with my house." And in 1916 came a cinema design—a stark, striking building done in simple geometric planes of reinforced concrete—which was so visually startling that it was dubbed "a warehouse for potatoes, an ice house, a cellar for cheese."

Several other revolutionary schemes produced by Le Corbusier during this early period escaped harsh criticism probably only because they stayed on the drawing board instead of suddenly appearing on the street. One was the Maison Domino, a house with an ultra-smooth reinforced-concrete frame intended for postwar construction. Like "domino blocks," the houses could be mass-produced and put together in all sorts of interesting combinations. It would probably strike us as a simple, even commonplace, design today, because prefabricated houses of every sort have cropped up everywhere during the past half century. But in 1914 few had ever really thought of "housing" as separate and distinct from "houses." The Maison Domino was just a core of a house, really—two floors, a roof, and a stairway. It was flexible, standardized, and inexpensive to build. The tenant could add furnishings, equipment, and slab or glass partitions as he or she pleased.

Another radical plan was for a city hoisted high on pylons or pillars in order to separate pedestrian from vehicular traffic. This was the first example of the reversal technique for which Corbu was to become famous: by using reinforced concrete he could have gardens on roofs, where one would least expect them, and only clear green space and vehicles on the ground, where one would expect gardens.

Of the seven buildings he had completed by the time he was thirty, the one that best summarized Le Corbusier's development was the Villa Schwob, completed in 1916. It contained many of the features the architect was to incorporate time and time again in later projects: a concrete frame (one of the first in Europe), a small flat-roof garden, columns (four interior ones around the central living room, allowing space to flow freely from one room to the next), internal variation in height (the living room carried through two stories), natural lighting (the living room was lit by a huge vertical window), a clear logical separation between the communal functional room on the public ground floor and the private rooms above, a rigorous but simplified geometrical design, and the use of "regulating lines"—a way of utilizing proportional triangles to achieve the harmony and order Corbu thought was essential to all architectural beauty.

The clients for the Villa Schwob and Corbu's other projects of this period were mostly wealthy, self-made leaders of industry—the kind he was to search for in vain as the years progressed. But Le Corbusier didn't appreciate them when he had them. He complained about their narrowmindedness and their unwillingness to take a chance on new and exciting forms. One of his letters reveals his dissatisfaction: "It seems to me clear that they don't want me any more, because in the end, my utter scrupulousness disgusts the people [of La Chaux-de-Fonds]. One has to be conceited, sanctimonious, sure of oneself, swaggering and never doubting—or at least not let it show. One has to be like a show salesman."

Finally Corbu could take his countrymen no longer. "The Swiss are clean, and industrious, and to hell with them," he said as he packed his bag. With an invitation from the city of Frankfurt, Germany, to do some municipal building, and a newly obtained passport in his pocket, he suddenly changed his mind and headed for Paris—"the city that can never be wrong . . . a monster of the most primitive kind." From that moment on, France was his home; thirteen years later he became a naturalized citizen. For the man who secretly considered himself a genius, only Paris could provide a worthy backdrop.

Villa Years

In Paris, Le Corbusier set himself up in a place that he described as a "servant's room, seventh floor, over a yard, in a beastly little street." For seventeen years he occupied these cramped quarters on the city's Left Bank.

His early hope was to pioneer a mass-production industry. For years he experimented with one concrete system after another, but all were doomed to failure. His romantic, exciting dreams collided with harsh realities or, as he phrased it, "economic shipwreck."

His poor financial condition had telling physical effects. Photographs taken at this time show a much thinner Le Corbusier, one with pursed lips and a stern, intense, almost glacial gaze. Although he was often broke and was almost exclusively in the company of simple, down-to-earth people like craftsmen, Corbu tried to maintain a middle-class style. His starched wing collar, bow tie, and dark business suit became as familiar as his heavy horn-rimmed glasses.

One morning, the abstract painter Fernand Leger and a friend sat in an outdoor café in Paris. Suddenly the friend looked at his watch and said to Leger, "Just wait. You're about to see a very odd specimen. He goes bicycling in a derby hat."

"A few minutes later," Leger recalled, "I saw coming along, very stiff, completely in silhouette, an extraordinary mobile object under the derby hat, with spectacles and a dark suit. He advanced quietly, scrupulously obeying the laws of perspective. The picturesque personage was none other than the architect Le Corbusier."

Corbu probably deserved the comment Auguste Perret made upon introducing him to the cubist painter Amédée Ozenfant: "He's a very curious bird, Amédée, but he will interest you."

As it turned out, the interest was mutual. The two had much in common. Born a year before Le Corbusier, Ozenfant was the son of a construction company owner who was a pioneer in advanced building techniques. "We admired, both of us equally, the masterpieces of modern industry," wrote the painter. Like Corbu, Ozenfant was fascinated by the new products of industry—airplanes and grain silos—and had even designed a streamlined chassis for a Hispano-Suiza auto in 1912.

The two also had a common writing style: an evangelical mode like that of Wright (who nevertheless dismissed Corbu as "that painter and pamphleteer" and once refused him admission to Taliesin on the grounds that "I don't see journalists"). The painter had edited an avant-garde magazine for a year, and Le Corbusier had authored three books (in the pattern he was to adhere to ever afterwards: setting forth an expected criticism and then defending his position in crisp staccato sentences, often filled with misspelled words and poor punctuation).

Corbu and Ozenfant became inseparable friends. Le Corbusier even began to paint—the "guitar, bottle, and pipe" kind of art popular then. The two promulgated their ideas in a lively magazine called *L'Esprit Nouveau,* which they published along with a poet friend for more than three years. Its most important articles were those on architecture, which Ozenfant and Corbu sometimes authored together. The articles were signed "Le Corbusier-Saugnier" to signify that Corbu did the writing while Ozenfant supplied the photos and sometimes the theme. Saugnier was an ancestral name of the Ozenfants, and Le Corbusier was a family name of the Jeannerets. The architect adopted the name Le Corbusier in the hope of establishing a separate and distinct identity in the architectural profession. It means "crow," which he is said to have resembled in profile, and which he began using as a personal insignia in his letters and on other occasions.

The two friends still signed their articles on paintings as Ozenfant and Jeanneret, however. And Le Corbusier also used the pen name of Paul Boulard. These pseudonyms are an indication of the complexity of the man and the broad range of his talents. In the mornings, as Charles-Edouard Jeanneret, he painted his still lifes; in the afternoons, as Le Corbusier, he turned to architectural design; and in the evenings, as either Jeanneret, Le Corbusier, or Boulard, he penned his books and articles.

But the situation was confusing, to say the least. Even the two principals eventually got mixed up. Le Corbusier accused his partner of changing dates on several paintings to give the impression he had had an idea a year before Le Corbusier. Ozenfant pouted that the joint signature "Le Corbusier-Saugnier" led many to believe he had a mistress named "Le Corbusier." Then, in 1923, came the book *Towards a New Architecture*, which was largely a compilation of the architecture articles that had appeared in their magazine. The first edition, which bore the hybrid name Le Corbusier-Saugnier, achieved immediate worldwide attention. Le Corbusier felt that Ozenfant was receiving too much credit for the authorship and omitted the name Saugnier on the second edition. He also added a dedication to Ozenfant.

"The fellow thanked me for the dedication," Corbu recalled later with a mischievous grin. "He didn't realize that by printing it, I had prevented anyone from thinking he'd written the book."

Recriminations and jealousy grew. Eventually the magazine folded, and the two one-time friends parted in bitterness. Ozenfant added insult to injury by presenting a check to Le Corbusier for services to his magazine. The sum was so meager that the recipient, who always bore grudges tenaciously anyway, kept it forever in his pocket to pull out and exhibit in order to discredit his former partner. The association had lasted seven years, longer than most for Le Corbusier.

The appearance of *Towards a New Architecture* in 1923 did

more than precipitate the split-up. It marked a turning point in the life of the Swiss-born rebel, who stopped using the name Jeanneret altogether, as well as all his other pseudonyms except Le Corbusier. He decided that he was first and foremost an architect, not a painter. And he even refused to show any more of his art; none was shown until 1937.

The book proclaimed a brave new world of construction— "Our eyes are made to see forms in light: cubes, cones, spheres, cylinders or pyramids are the great primary forms." To illustrate, it presented photos of American ocean liners, bridges, grain elevators, and docks. It contained one of the most beautiful and widely quoted definitions of architecture: "the masterly, correct and magnificent play of masses brought together in light."

It preached the basic dictum "A house is a machine for living in," which was hung, like an albatross, around Le Corbusier's neck from then on. Taken out of context, the statement was the basis for labeling him a functionalist in the most austere, arid sense. This was unfair, for almost in the same breath he said, "Passion can create drama out of inert stone" and "Art has no business resembling a machine." And later, "Art has the sole duty to move us." The point he was trying to get across was that a house should be at least as practical and efficient as a typewriter, telephone, or airplane. But it was beauty, humanity, passion—not utilitarianism—that constituted art in his eyes.

He published three other key books between 1921 and 1925, all of them composed of articles from *L'Esprit Nouveau,* for he had written about ten thousand words a month during these prolific years with the magazine. Embracing a wide spectrum of subjects—architecture, urbanism, industrial design, and painting—and translated into several languages, they were more effective propaganda than his buildings proved to be.

It's difficult to believe that the author of these cocksure revolutionary books had barely any actual building to his credit when they appeared—just a few early structures at La Chaux-de-Fonds, a studio-house for Ozenfant, and a villa at Vanererson. But he was working, writing, dreaming, and preparing all the time. In 1921 he and a young cousin, Pierre Jeanneret, opened an architectural studio at 35, rue de Sèvres on the Left Bank of Paris. It was nothing more than a short, walled-off section on the second floor of a Jesuit monastery. But it provided the architect with the solitude and simplicity he always considered essential to creativity.

Here he drew his plans for the Ville Contemporaine, a "City for Three Million Inhabitants." The mechanics of urban life had been a major concern of his since 1910, when he wrote a paper on the town planning of his native city. This contemporary city scheme contained, in essence, the architect's concept of an ideal urban center. Features of the plan would run through all his future projects. In all, before his death he was to be responsible for designs for many different cities—Algiers (seven plans altogether), Stockholm, Moscow, Buenos Aires, Montevideo, Rio de Janeiro, Paris, Zurich, Antwerp, Barcelona, New York, Bogota, the war-destroyed city of Saint-Dié, La Rochelle-Pallice, Marseilles, and Chandigarh. Of all these, only one—Chandigarh—was actually built by the architect.

Le Corbusier was not a city planner by training, and when he came upon the scene, no city had been "designed" for a hundred years. Yet he saw immediately the necessity for bringing the city into the province of architecture. For him, city planning and architecture were inseparable. What is the use, he asked himself, of designing beautiful, efficient houses if they must rise on the streets of ugly, outdated urban relics?

What's so remarkable is that Corbu's principles of city planning had such a pervasive influence on urban environments everywhere. The influence was indirect, of course, for he was never to hold any official planning post except in India, and he was to be denied one urban design commission after the other. Even his interest in the problem was largely self-generated and was sustained only by his own initiative. Yet he, more than any other architect of his time, is most vividly associated with urbanism. He, more than any other, directed the attention of the younger generation to the importance of planning cities. Though in the 1920s traffic was hardly the monumental problem that it is today, he was the first (with his elevated buildings and lifted highways) to develop and defend the complete separation of vehicular and pedestrian traffic.

Let's look at his dreams for the city as they were first set down over fifty years ago. At the center of Corbu's "City of Three Million" was a group of cross-shaped skyscrapers, fifty to sixty stories high. Widely spaced in expanses of greenery like "towers in a park," these were to house the administrative, business, and professional offices. Beyond the central ring was a civic and cultural center, and then a series of belts of apartment houses, each twelve stories or six double stories high, and each possessing its own garden. Beyond a several-mile-wide green belt (designed to protect and isolate the city forever) were the industrial districts, a great sports arena, farms, a suburb of individual houses, and perhaps a port. Elevated highways, never used by walkers, crisscrossed the city to make the center quickly and easily accessible. On the outskirts, these roadways were joined by a highway system that completely bypassed the built-up area. There was also an airstrip for air traffic. Under the buildings on stilts, pedestrians could walk freely and unafraid. When the city population reached three million, new cities should be built to accommodate the excess growth, proclaimed Le Corbusier.

This bold proposition was openly attacked from the moment of its exhibition in 1922. Nevertheless, such novel projects and buildings were drawing young apprentice architects from all over the globe to Le Corbusier's studio in Paris. There they found him, behind a door labeled with a forbidding "Keep Out" sign, kept company mainly by a black cocker.

He was working, finally, for his first major client—one of the class he referred to as "enlightened businessmen" or "managerial elite"— a Swiss banker named Raoul La Roche. On a tight, narrow lot, Corbu had to construct a house for La Roche and one for his musician brother Albert. (Today this is the Foundation Le Corbusier, chief research center for studies about the architect.) He solved the problem ingeniously: the lighting and the layering of punched-out flat surfaces provide an illusion of continuous space. There was an "architectural promenade" to highlight the La Roche collection of paintings—a triple-height entrance hall ending either in a ramped gallery (Corbu's first use of the ramp) or an open-air roof garden, depending on your chosen route.

A year or two later he built a long, low villa for his mother on the shores of Lac Lemon in Switzerland, where she lived until her death in 1951. It was a charming, unpretentious home. Even the traditional Swiss furniture and artifacts seemed to fit the modern setting. But the municipal officials still announced, "This house is a crime against nature; it must never happen again."

By this time Le Corbusier was beginning to expect such a response, but even he wasn't prepared for what ensued when he was invited to participate in the International Exhibition of Decorative Arts in Paris in 1925. First, he was given the worst possible site, one practically outside the exhibition area. Undaunted, Corbu and cousin Pierre built the Pavilion de l'Esprit Nouveau, a full-sized concrete model of the "superimposed villas" developed a few years earlier for the contemporary city. The idea was to show that such a pavilion could actually be built. Simple, small, and economical, it was a hollow court with a two-story apartment inside and a two-story living room within that. It was a radical approach to architecture. Gone was the traditional facade, with its two-dimensional arrangement of windows on a wall, and its inner space bottled up in cubicles.

Le Corbusier filled this strange "apartment" with even stranger furnishings, some of his own designing: chromium-plated tubular steel furniture; built-in units now called storage walls, which were then seen only in offices; paintings; and objects such as beach pebbles, laboratory utensils, and airplane models, added to "evoke poetic reactions." What the architect was offering was a strictly utilitarian place for living, stripped bare to go with the spirit of a new age. His loud and clear statement was that furnishings should equip, not adorn—a startling proclamation in an exhibition whose theme was "decorative arts." But then, Corbu never worried about such details.

As if all this weren't shocking enough, the architect added an annex to his pavilion in which he displayed his Plan Voisin, his "contemporary city" scheme applied to the city of Paris. This was a proposal for razing an area of Paris roughly to the northeast of the Louvre and modernizing it with skyscrapers, apartment blocks, highways, and a railroad station topped by an airport. It was the first urban renewal plan suggested for the city since one drawn up for Napoleon in the 1860s. Corbu called it Plan Voisin because, with typical audacity, he had convinced Gabriel Voisin, the automobile manufacturer, that he should finance the project. (Car makers Peugeot and Citroen had already turned him down.)

"It's your motorcars helping to cause the urban traffic jams," he told Voisin, "so you should support my attempts at a solution." Naturally the Parisians didn't take kindly to this proposed demolition of the heart of their beloved city. The weekly magazine *Arts* screamed "Megalomania! Vandalism! Vanity! Monotony!" Other self-appointed critics shouted "too costly and crazy!" The officials of the exhibition even constructed a high fence around the pavilion and its annex, hoping to keep visitors away altogether. Only the intercession of a cabinet minister got it torn down. Then, when the international jury boldly decided to award Corbu first prize, the French member of the group successfully vetoed the vote on the grounds that the pavilion "contained no architecture." Groaned the architect, "In Paris, prophets are kicked in the rear."

All the uproar must have convinced him he'd have a better chance writing about cities, since apparently no one was about to let him build them. So on the bookstands appeared his next work, *Urbanisme*. In it, he appealed for the emergence of idealistic "captains of industry," who, like Louis XIV, would issue the command for a city to be rebuilt in one stroke.

On a smaller scale, one such patron did pop up almost immediately—Henri Fruges, heir to his father's sugar factory. Won over by the author-architect's goals, this altruistic businessman commissioned Le Corbusier to construct a model workers' city near Bordeaux. In the box-like white houses (often described as sugar cubes) were economical, standardized windows, staircases, and heating and kitchen equipment. To avoid the monotony customary in mass housing Corbu varied the make-up in the units. Much space was left open to allow for individualization and flexibility in both use and construction.

None of this impressed local bureaucrats. They went to even

greater lengths to sabotage this latest Corbu project. Offended by the geometrical open and closed cubes, authorities delayed signing the necessary occupancy permits. As the architect later observed wryly, the buildings took only one year to construct but three years to be occupied—thanks to the deliberate snarling of bureaucratic red tape.

As some compensation for such abuse, however, Le Corbusier was finally getting the opportunity to build; private villas sprang up in the leafy Parisian suburbs like some alien objects from outer space. Three stand out particularly: the Cook house at Burlogne-sur-Seine (1926); the Villa Stein at Garches (1927); and the Villa Savoye at Poissy, designed in 1929 and completed two years later. All were elaborations of Corbu's basic theme: the hollowed-out cube (the "pure prism") hoisted high on columns and crowned with a roof garden. All were good early examples of his "plastic" style, in which houses resembled sculpture. All were objects of intense curiosity in their immediate neighborhoods, and they attracted more interest, discussion, and fame around the world than any other houses of the century.

In the Cook house, the first floor held an open terrace and parking area, the second floor contained all the bedrooms and baths, and the third and fourth floors held the living areas—Le Corbusier's customary reversal trick at work again. Most startling were its freely curving partitions. One partition was shaped like an elongated S to accommodate a grand piano; another was molded to fit a lozenge-shaped bathtub. In both the Cook house and the Stein villa, the short end walls were blank or almost blank, an interesting contrast to the long, open, glassy facade. Quite by accident, these blank end walls became synonymous with certain kinds of modern architecture and almost a Corbu trademark. Actually, he left them blank because he always felt he was building units of a larger whole rather than independent entities.

The Villa Stein at Garches, regarded as sort of a landmark in Le Corbusier's career, influenced architects the world over with its gracefully sculptured stairs, suspended canopies, and continuous ribbon windows; its interesting interplay of levels and forms; and its use of the well-known "golden section" system of proportions to provide unity and harmony. (Corbu later invented his own system, the modulor.) The huge roofed gallery is reminiscent of a big ocean liner (which indeed often inspired the architect) or an awesome white rectangular box.

It is the Villa Savoye in Paris, completed in 1931, that stands out as the architect's most important and unique house. It marked him indelibly as the creative genius he was. Rising above the grassy fields of Poissy, overlooking the valley of the Seine, this pure white box on delicate stilts was the culmination of the early phase of the builder's career.

The Villa Savoye incorporated Corbu's "five points" on a much larger, more luxurious, and more architecturally sophisticated scale. And there were, additionally, other characteristic elements: the entrance ramp, the curving walls of the solarium, and the column and slab construction. By setting the ground floor back to provide room for a car to pass, and by curving the way to accord with the minimum turning circle of a car, Le Corbusier became the first to create a home for a "fully motorized family." An automobile, having unloaded its passengers at the main entrance, could continue down the other side of the building, still under cover of the floor above, and leave by a road parallel to the approaching one.

Frank Lloyd Wright dismissed this villa as just a "box on stilts." English architectural critic and historian Reyner Banham said, " . . . the effect of these curved forms, standing on a square slab raised on legs, is like nothing so much as a still-life arranged on a table." Others called it an alien space capsule touched down on the landscape.

For many people around the world, however, it was the epitome of new, modern architecture, and its creator was invited to lecture in such major capitals as Moscow, Sao Paulo, Algiers, Stockholm, Barcelona, Brussels, and Prague.

Le Corbusier was also building in Germany during this era. In 1927 the German Werkbund was sponsoring an international housing exhibition in Stuttgart. Mies van der Rohe, who was exhibition director, asked Le Corbusier and Pierre Jeanneret to design two experimental buildings. Corbu accepted the

Stuttgart invitation for two reasons. First, Mies offered him his choice of site (as Mies recalled later, "Naturally he chose the best."). Second, Corbu knew that the sponsoring Werkbund strongly favored the fusion of art and modern industrialized architecture, which Le Corbusier planned to carry out in his two building entries.

Characteristically, he seized the opportunity to make the exhibition a soap box for his convictions. His now famous houses were launched with a manifesto in the architect's crisp, chip-on-the-shoulder style: "This is by no means an aesthetic fantasy or a search for fashionable effects; we are dealing with architectural facts which call for an absolutely new way of building." Then Le Corbusier's "five points" were tabulated— the columns, the roof garden, the free plan, the long windows, and the free facade. These Corbusier standards were to become part of the vocabulary of the modern movement.

The exhibition buildings were an exact realization of Corbu's standards: one was a precisely and beautifully proportioned cube on stilts, and the other was a portion of what we might term a garden-apartment unit. The apartment house's partitions were all prefabricated storage walls, and the furniture, other than chairs and tables, was completely built in.

The clients who gave the architect the chance to bring to fruition all the purist notions and architectural principles he'd been developing for the past ten years were a breed apart. As might be expected, they were enlightened men, wealthy enough to be able to afford the experimental architecture. He expected them to realize that his buildings were there to make a point or express a theory and so would be anything but cozy and comfortable.

Clients adjusted best by accepting their role as "animated footnotes." So what if bedrooms were as cramped as sleeping car compartments on a train, or if children's quarters were too far away from parents for peace of mind? Two examples typify the architect's somewhat disdainful attitude toward those who occupied his buildings. Le Corbusier built a studio for his friend, sculptor Jacques Lipchitz. "A good studio," remarks Lipchitz, "but he would not allow me to put any of my sculptures along the walls." When one tenant complained that her roof leaked and invited Corbu to come see for himself, he accepted her invitation and then proceeded to nonchalantly sail paper boats in the puddles on the floor.

While the Villa Savoye was under construction, Le Corbusier was also building an amazing penthouse apartment on the Champs-Elysées. The roof terrace was furnished with imitation stone furniture, grass carpet, and fake daisies. The precisely clipped, geometric boxwood hedges which rimmed the terrace slipped out of sight on an electric elevator at the push of a button. Walls also moved by electricity. Yet the lighting came from candles reflected in mirrors.

With plants that could pop up or down at man's will, the architect demonstrated his victory over nature. All of his early buildings were openly and obviously man-made, standing on pillars tall above the landscape. No one could be farther away from Wright, who used natural materials and built horizontally, trying to ease his buildings into their settings and smudge the distinction between them and the landscape. The American preferred organic growth; the Frenchman, an arithmetic process. Wright felt more; Le Corbusier thought more. Their differences stemmed from their backgrounds and basic philosophies. Wright was of the New World and was inspired by the Orient. He was a country boy who built more for the individual, the family. He was more prolific than Le Corbusier, and all his buildings had a sympathy with nature, a romantic element. Corbu, a city slicker at heart, was European and was influenced by the Mediterranean. More coldly analytical, he designed in defiance of nature. Instead of melting into the background, his surprising and unnatural building materials stood out boldly.

Corbu's synthetic materials—concrete, glass, and strong paint—shone brilliantly. But they required a perfect finish to retain their effectiveness. The pure white glass and stucco skins of Le Corbusier's 1920s villas did not weather well. Rain chipped and streaked them. This was just one of the reasons why, in the next phase of his career, he turned more and more toward nature.

Expanding Horizons

The year 1929 marked the end of what Le Corbusier called his first period of investigation. And 1930 opened for him a new period of new tasks—"important works, great events in architecture and city planning, to the marvelous epoch of evolving a new machine civilization."

It was, in Corbu's mind, time to build big. The decade of the 1930s was indeed marked by giant projects, but most of them never got off the paper they were planned on.

These projects included plans for the League of Nations building at Geneva, the Centrosoyus building in Moscow, the Salvation Army building in Paris, the Pavilion Suisse for the Cité Universitaire in Paris, the Rentenanstalt building in Zurich, an apartment house and skyscrapers in Algiers, and a Ministry of Education and Public Health in Rio de Janeiro, among many others.

Four got off the drawing board: the Moscow structure, the Salvation Army building, the Swiss Pavilion, and the ministry in Rio. But all the designs showed that the architect had developed a hunger for grandiose vistas, a love for sensations of limitless space, and a craving for the vast horizon.

In these same years, proposals for shaping or reshaping major cities also came from his studio. He planned new designs for Paris, Algiers, Barcelona, Antwerp, Stockholm, and New York. In them, he very clearly showed a shift from the straight line to more curvilinear forms—unexpected from the man who not many years earlier had damned the curve as "the pack donkey's way."

This loosening up, this completely new openness was apparent not only in city plans and public buildings but in his domestic architecture as well. Increasingly he turned to more traditional, natural building materials: rough timber, broken stone, exposed brick, raw concrete, and industrial materials left "as found." Increasingly he constructed in the materials of primitive societies.

Instead of the urbane, formal, and sophisticated home, Le Corbusier began to produce a more personal one. Spaces and masses opened up in his villas. A new subservience to nature was revealed in houses that hugged the earth instead of standing dominantly upright. Roof gardens were abandoned, and more restful interiors created. Fireplaces helped anchor his houses more firmly to the ground.

In his public buildings, apartment houses, and office buildings, the customary flat roof line of the 1920s was replaced by a more complex roof superstructure (such as the sculptured forms atop his Marseilles block). So while the roof garden slowly disappeared from his private houses between 1929 and 1945, it acquired a new importance in his public structures. And the relationship between the public space on the rooftop and the natural surroundings was definitely established. Another change that suddenly appeared about 1933, on a proposed apartment house for Algiers, was the brise-soleil or sun-breaker—a sort of visor or venetian blind that was to become a Corbu trademark.

The architect's rediscovery of nature during this period is nowhere more vividly affirmed than in a letter he wrote in 1936 to a group of young South Africans:

"How are we to enrich our creative powers? Not by subscribing to architectural reviews, but by undertaking voyages of discovery into the inexhaustible domain of nature. . . . I wish that architects would sometimes take up their pencils to draw a plant or a leaf—or to express the significance of the clouds, the ever-changing ebb and flow of waves at play upon the sands. . . ."

If Frank Lloyd Wright had read these words of Corbu, he might have recognized a kindred soul and abandoned his slander of that "box-builder and pamphleteer."

The numerous alterations in Corbu's style resulted from a reappraisal of his 1920s work, which wasn't weathering well, and a deeper reflection on nature. But the new openness and broadening of horizons were probably a result of changes occurring in his private life, too. In 1930 he became a citizen of the country he loved and had adopted—France. About the same time he began to travel widely. New worlds opened on the home front, too, when in 1930 he married vivacious, dark-eyed Yvonne Gallis. A Monaco-born fashion model, she was introduced to Corbu by the painter Ozenfant in 1922. They lived together for several years before persuasion from Yvonne and, no doubt, Le Corbusier's Swiss Protestant family resulted in the conventional legal union. Not an intellectual and not at all interested in architecture, she accorded her architect-husband treatment that was in sharp contrast to the awe and respect he received at his studio.

"All this light is killing me, driving me crazy," she said when he designed an apartment with a glass curtain wall for her. And when he wouldn't leave his work at her call, she'd appear, hands on hips, at his studio door, admonishing, "Mr. Modulor, your lunch is getting cold." She was a great companion—the simple, down-to-earth kind of person Le Corbusier always preferred. Her sharp wit and bawdy humor often broke up the solemn meetings of the august architectural groups to which her husband belonged. They were together for thirty-six years until her death in 1957, but no sons or daughters appeared. Le Corbusier once explained why: "When I was married, I said to my wife 'no children' because I feared at that time that my life would be very hard as an architect."

Again Corbu was prophesying correctly. One of the hardest disappointments came in 1927, with the architectural competition for the League of Nations building. The Le Corbusier entry was doomed from the start. Corbu later wrote bitterly of the incident: "After sixty-five meetings of the jury in Geneva, the project of L-C and Pierre Jeanneret was the only one of three hundred and sixty schemes (seven miles of plans) that received four votes out of nine. It was at this point that the delegate from Paris pointed out: 'This scheme has not been drawn in India ink. I insist it be disqualified.' And it was."

The jury compromised by awarding *nine first prizes,* one of them to Corbu, and asking the League's political heads to choose one of the nine for the actual job. The politicians chose four, not one, traditionalists in the neoclassical vein; for two years these four argued over a design. In the meantime the site was changed, and Corbu-Jeanneret submitted a second entry to fit the new site.

When the four traditionalists finally settled on a design, it differed noticeably from the conservative entry originally sub-mitted in 1927. And it bore a remarkable resemblance to Le Corbusier's plan. Never a good loser, Corbu ordered an attor-ney to submit a thirty-six-page brief to the League charging piracy of the design. A five-line reply came back: the organiza-tion could not concern itself with individual complaints.

As happened not infrequently, Le Corbusier had to watch as others took his design and applied it successfully. Again he was paying the price for being first. The wedge-shaped assembly hall in his League of Nations plan was the result of considerable effort. He wanted to assure the twenty-six hundred participants in world government an adequate sight line and an adequate acoustic line. Today this innovation is standard in every well-designed meeting hall. Some small consolation came to the architect about 1939, when the University of Zurich purchased his original League plans to hang as a work of art.

But of even greater satisfaction was the effect the episode had on modern architecture. The League contest was the most important international design competition of the time, and Le Corbusier's entry was the first serious challenge leveled by a modernist at the old guard academicians. At the same time that his design was being declared ineligible on a technicality, a newspaper was attacking Corbu's work in a Swiss town neighboring La Chaux-de-Fonds. All this commotion and con-troversy focused world attention on modern architecture. No longer was it viewed as just another passing fancy, but as a serious, sustained movement.

The League jury's shabby treatment of Le Corbusier also

gave a new unified fighting spirit to those who shared his convictions. This led to the formation of CIAM (Congrès Internationaux d'Architecture Moderne)—an organization of modernists from all countries, dedicated to protecting and informing its members, and to exerting influence through the members' work and schools.

The League rejection and the newspaper attack were typical of what the leaders of modern architecture had to endure all through the 1930s and early 1940s. Le Corbusier realized that, as one of the best known and most outspoken of these leaders, he would have to bear the brunt of the attack. But it never stopped hurting.

Despite the pain, Le Corbusier always leaped right back into the fire. Never above a kind of architectural street fighting, he would immediately launch a counterattack by publishing an answering pamphlet or book, or designing another revolutionary building. Still smarting from the League of Nations fiasco, for example, he came right back with another international project to be situated next to the League's center—the Mundaneum, or "Centre of Centres." This world city or world communications center was an architectural response to a brainstorm of Belgian industrialist Paul Otlet (christened "Saint Paul" by Corbu for his efforts to spread the gospel). Otlet's aim was to promote international understanding through peace and through progress founded on broad humanitarian ideals. Le Corbusier translated the aim into a plan for a world library, university, stadium, and museum. It was another Corbu design destined never to see the light of day, but both the architect and Otlet wasted a lot of time and money staging lectures and exhibitions in an effort to stir up interest in their utopian project.

One of the architect's designs did get built in Geneva about this time, however. It was the Immeuble Charte (or the Glass House, as it is called locally)—a building of forty-five apartments. Even the double-story living rooms and the built-in furnishings were constructed entirely of standardized elements. The Immeuble Charte is one of three or four buildings in which Le Corbusier used glass walls extensively.

Then came the chance to construct a really large-scale

design—Le Corbusier's largest to date. It was the Centrosoyus (Cooperative) building in Moscow (now the Building for the Ministry of Light Industry), a monolithic office block for thirty-five hundred workers. Plans for the compound were sent to Moscow in 1929. A shortage of building materials, however, delayed completion until 1933. The complex was extremely open—long blocks of offices and a fan-shaped assembly hall were linked together by sculptured, sweeping ramps. It was the last significant building to go up in Russia before a shift back to ornamental architecture. But one extremely advanced feature Le Corbusier intended it to have—air-conditioning—never materialized. The architect wasn't on the site to supervise, and the cautious Russians substituted an orthodox radiator heating system instead. This dealt with the cold Moscow winters but completely ignored the sweltering summers.

His attempts to air-condition his next building, a giant office block for the Salvation Army, were also thwarted. Several years earlier Le Corbusier had built his first communal structure— the Palais du Peuple—for the Salvation Army. And he had paid tribute to the group in one of his books for having taught its members the proper way to live. So he was particularly gratified to get two more commissions from the organization in 1929. One was for a ship—L'Asile Flottant or the Floating Asylum—that was to provide winter shelter for shivering down-and-outers and streetwalkers, and summer recreation for the poor children of Paris. The other was for an eight-story asylum on land, although the final version resembled a ship in plan, profile, interior, and operation. (Corbu had long admired the ocean liner, and was probably the first theoretician to use it as a model not only of good design, but also of an ideal way of life.)

The land structure, called the City of Refuge, boasted a gigantic doorway crowned with a cantilevered canopy, elaborate interior ramps for both pedestrians and automobiles, a library, dining halls, dormitories, and something new— suspended rolling trolleys for window cleaning (the forerunner of those used on the New York Lever building twenty years later). A financial slump and foundation difficulties (piles had to be driven forty-five feet down through the underground waters of the Seine) delayed construction, but the narrow slab building finally opened in 1933.

Financial reverses also prevented the completion of Le Corbusier's air-conditioning plans. Dormitories overheated in summer, so window openings and sunbreakers were added, destroying the effect of the smooth, clear-glass facade. Corbu felt such "architectural mistakes," as he termed them, by the City of Refuge staff did more damage to his building than the German troops who later occupied it during the war. He stated that the structure could "no longer be thought of as architecture."

Even greater frustration was in store for him, though. Right after the revolution in Russia, socialist building programs had resulted in much experimental and modern construction. Le Corbusier had been studying the Russian constructivists and, in 1928, had even put up a building that owed much to them: the butterfly-roofed Nestlé Pavilion, which, with its blown-up graphics and chocolate products, was virtually a collage of advertisement. His plans for the Palace of the Soviets followed this same modern line. He may even have surpassed the Russians in the game of structural gymnastics. Two wedge-shaped main assembly halls for fifteen thousand spectators were slung from riblike girders that resembled the jagged saw-teeth of a shark. The reinforced-concrete roof of the Great Hall, suspended from a huge parabolic arch, formed an acoustically perfect shell. Beneath the auditorium, with its stage for fifteen hundred performers, its foyers, its lounges, its restaurants, its accommodations for diplomatic corps and press, and its technically advanced backstage fittings, was a huge cloakroom where coats, overshoes, and gloves could be stored and dried. This was a brainstorm of practicality in such a cold, snowy country. To satisfy the post-revolution mania for mass celebration and gigantic spectacles, there was an open-air platform for fifty thousand. The whole complex of skeletal structures provided a dramatic clash of dark glass and white volumes. Surrounding it was an automobile circuit that gave access to all parts of the building and completely separated pedestrians from cars.

But a Soviet jury rejected the design as "looking too much like a factory." The Palace was built in the Italian Renaissance style, and Corbu's remarkable model got nowhere—except to an exhibition at the Museum of Modern Art in New York in 1935, and then on a tour of several American cities.

Understandably embittered by this episode, the architect almost turned down the next commission offered to him. It was to build the hostel for Swiss students at the Cité Universitaire in the south of Paris. Still smarting from the degrading treatment he'd received from his native countrymen in the League of Nations incident, Le Corbusier was only persuaded to accept the job after pressure from the combined universities of Switzerland. Fortunately he did, for the result was a milestone in his development and in the history of modern architecture. This simple building of great originality is often said to have turned Corbu into a world figure almost overnight.

Completed in 1932 at the modest cost of three million francs, the Swiss Pavilion encompasses in a single structure all the elements of new construction that Corbu had been tentatively trying out in such buildings as the Villa Savoye and the Soviet Palace. In fact, it is sometimes called one of the first truly modern buildings. The architect himself described it as "a veritable laboratory of modern architecture"—he was probably thinking mainly of such technical innovations as dry-wall construction, internal plumbing, and acoustic separation (insulation). All through the 1930s students from far and near visited this beautiful dormitory like a shrine.

This disarmingly simple and pure four-story "vertical slab" is cantilevered out from its columns one floor above the ground. It is a symphony of contrasts—the blank end walls versus the glass-filled panels on the long side; the pure prism of the upper steel-framed slab versus the bulk of the massively sculpted concrete columns below (no longer the sensual, slender stilts used in the 1920s); and the curved rubblestone wall on the ground floor versus the smooth stone veneer finish on the building proper.

Interestingly enough, the curved wall of the pavilion's common room or library came eventually to be the canvas for a long floor-to-ceiling mural painted by Le Corbusier. It was one of his finest examples of cubism, in the tradition of the earlier Picasso.

The year after the dedication ceremony for the Swiss Pavilion, which Corbu described as more like a funeral than a celebration, a competition for the design of an insurance company headquarters was announced in Zurich. Still a glutton for punishment, Le Corbusier submitted an entry. You can guess what happened: it was disqualified at once. Of course, the architect had immediately discarded the promoters' plan as backward and inappropriate to the site. The client's preconception was of a low building with a central courtyard. "Too spreading for the available ground dimensions," pronounced Corbu, "and ignorant of new techniques in planning and construction." He proposed instead a ten-story office block designed with modern functions in mind—heating, air-conditioning, and built-in services. For example, it was lozenge-shaped in order to accommodate the extra space required by the elevator core.

Side by side with such large-scale buildings as the insurance headquarters, Le Corbusier was still designing private homes occasionally. And they all revealed his new interest in primitive building materials. Even Le Corbusier's own studio-apartment, occupying two floors of a building he designed in 1933 at 24, rue Nungesser-et-Coli in Paris, had walls of rough brick and concrete block.

In the architect's city plans of this period, there was a growing fluidity of line and form. Le Corbusier's output of city schemes between 1929 and 1945 was staggering. But they remained mostly theoretical experiments, and in a way were a form of self-torture. Few were commissioned or paid for, and all were rejected—either by juries in competitions or by local authorities. Yet Corbu kept trying again and again, painstakingly working out each dream in great detail on paper.

Le Corbusier studied the problem of urban expansion in Rio de Janeiro as early as 1929 during a lecture tour to South America. He designed a town plan for Rio as well as for the other cities he visited (Sao Paulo, Montevideo, and Buenos Aires), but all his South American ideas were turned down.

Undaunted, the very next year he drafted plans for the rebuilding of Algiers. It was the first of *seven* schemes for that city, culminating in the master plan he submitted to the Vichy government in 1942. This last was probably the best of his many paper projects for town building (except for the postwar plan for bombed-out Saint-Dié). It was a carefully studied, practical solution to a real problem—the typically crowded Mediterranean city. As part of the solution, Corbu ingeniously produced some brilliantly terraced buildings leading into continuous highways—a concept now being revived in many parts of the world. Again, rejection.

The same fate awaited two more of his city plans, submitted as competition entries in 1933. One for Antwerp, which called for a pedestrian central core bordered by superhighways, was judged "crazy stuff" and passed over for more down-to-earth proposals. One for Stockholm was considered by the jury for all of ten months—and then knocked down. In rapid succession, additional schemes of this period—one for Barcelona, another for Buenos Aires, and several for improving Paris—were turned down as fanciful and inhuman. "They are driving me away," the architect wrote. "They have closed the doors on me. I go and I feel this profoundly: 'I'm right, I'm right, I'm right.' . . . It is a bitter sorrow to see men devoted to their city stubbornly deny it the smile of art and the attitude of grandeur."

This hysterical tone was common in Corbu's writings before World War II. Later Le Corbusier calmed down, and was able to pen a more optimistic, though vindictive, note: "The defeat of these past years represents so many victories. Our rejected plans will become public accusers, for the public will judge the bureaucrats according to these plans; and the day will come when they will force a change."

At the heart of all these urban designs, from the very beginning, was Le Corbusier's tall tower, the skyscraper. No one else introduced it so convincingly as the new instrument for city building. Even his first plan, the 1922 Contemporary City, called for twenty-four of them—all fifty or sixty stories high—to form the core. Le Corbusier realized very early that he had to go up. Spreading out was too expensive, too wasteful, and too space consuming. Yet by 1935 the only skyscraper he had actually designed, the Rentenanstalt, was still on the drawing board. Although it was probably the best high-rise in the world and established the redeeming quality that was to become an essential for all high-rises—a wide carpet of space and greenery around the building—it was still only on paper.

So in 1935 it was with great anticipation that Corbu set off for New York and his first glimpse of its metropolitan towers. He had been invited to lecture there by the Museum of Modern Art in conjunction with an exhibition of his work. New Yorkers remembered the praise the architect had sung to America (sight unseen) as the epitome of machine art in his book *Towards a New Architecture*. They expected him to be dazzled when he first faced their buildings, and initially he was. "When I first saw the Empire State building," he told a friend in India many years afterward, "I wanted to lie down on my back right there on the sidewalk and gaze toward its top forever. A thousand feet high! That is an event in the history of architecture."

But admiration for technical skill did not blind Le Corbusier to defects. The more he traveled—from New York to Chicago to Detroit—the more convinced he became that skyscrapers were ruining American cities. It was bad enough to adorn the towers with decorative gimcracks and to consider height a virtue in itself. But even worse was the failure to use the towers properly as a part of wise city planning. To exploit land values, high-rise buildings were squeezed close together, cutting off light, view, and air, turning streets into canyons of dark corridors, Corbu charged. That Americans, who had really invented the skyscraper after all, should now allow it to victimize them was incomprehensible to Le Corbusier. And in his lectures, interviews, and debates around the country from late 1935 to early 1936, he told them so. "New York's skyscrapers are too small. . . . Central Park is too big. . . . The suburb is the great problem of the U.S.A. . . . Manhattan is so antagonistic to the fundamental needs of the human heart that the one idea of everybody is to escape. . . . All that remains is the dream. . . ." Speaking from a profound disillusionment, he told the truth as he saw it, bluntly and tactlessly, as usual.

Before long he was also embroiled in a financial battle with the Museum of Modern Art. As frugal as a Swiss shopkeeper,

Corbu was always accusing others of robbing him. He was receiving neither the amount of money nor the assistance from museum directors that he'd been promised, the architect accused. It was all a misunderstanding, but, needless to say, not too many Americans were sorry to see the crotchety critic leave their shores.

Back home in France, Corbu wrote *When the Cathedrals Were White,* which has been called "a charming lyrical love letter to America." But it was subtitled ominously "A Journey to the Country of Timid People." At any rate, the author did reaffirm his admiration for America's potentials and ask for a second chance to prove his affection. Many years and another bitter clash later, Le Corbusier finally got that chance and built his only United States building—the Harvard Carpenter Center of the Arts. (All of his foreign work was done with the least possible amount of traveling, so he never saw this building.)

In the meantime, the architect once again settled in his Paris studio, to fill more sheets with designs for tall structures that were never realized on land. It wasn't until 1945 that a high-rise designed and built by Corbu was actually completed. A Brazilian team headed by Lucio Costa and Oscar Niemayer asked Corbu to advise them on the design and construction of the new Ministry of Education building in Rio. Le Corbusier jumped at the chance to finally construct a skyscraper. Corbu, like all his other colleagues, was anxious to complete as much of his life's work as possible before the war, which was then imminent. He immediately flew to Rio and, instead of advising, virtually took over.

Costa, a modest and gracious gentleman, made it easy by withdrawing into the background. The building was totally Corbu's conception, but it is often attributed to Niemayer because a Brazilian law forbade payment to any foreign architect. To circumvent the absurd statute, Niemayer was officially placed in charge, while Le Corbusier, the real designer, received a swollen fee for lectures.

The seventeen-story building is the architect's largest prewar structure. Perched atop two-story cylindrical columns, the beautiful slab embodied all the standards Corbu had been developing and refining for many years: long, glassy side walls and blank end walls of a particularly splendid pink Brazilian granite; a ground-floor free-shaped assembly and exhibition hall slid under the top stories; a penthouse superstructure of restaurants and recreation areas; and a honeycomb of sun-control louvres.

The building dramatically changed the course of Brazilian architecture, as Costa graciously acknowledged in a letter written at the project's completion in 1945. And it has been the prototype for hundreds of similiar structures built since all over the world.

In the meantime, Corbu's other talents were not lying fallow. In his studio-apartment he painted both individual canvases and murals. His sculpture was exhibited in Zurich, and he contributed articles to magazines. He also added several more books to an already substantial publishing record. But architecture, his first love, still consumed most of his energies and attention.

As the world almost hypnotically watched the gradual build-up of Hitler's force and philosophy, Le Corbusier was still generating one startlingly creative project after the other.

Very early in life, Corbu had chosen reinforced concrete as his building material—partly because of its availability and economy, but mainly because of its flexibility. It was his clay, which he could mold and twist and shape into all the imaginative forms springing from his fertile mind. Yet there was always a simultaneous pull toward a building with steel and glass, inspired by the ocean liner, the automobile, and the airplane. He had even designed several mass-producible steel housing units and built two of them: one in Geneva in 1931, and a multistory apartment block in Paris (the penthouse of which he and his wife occupied) in 1934. These were, as one critic termed them, rather dry, monotonous and sterile, like much functionalist work of the period. But there was a kind of lyricism in the lightweight structure the architect built for the Paris World's Fair. This translucent tent was suspended above ramps and demonstration stands by steel cables and pylons.

Just as the architect was beginning to experiment with this

Frank Lloyd Wright at age
twenty. *Courtesy, State
Historical Society of
Wisconsin*

Martin House, Buffalo, New York, 1904.
Courtesy, Museum of Modern Art, New York

Kaufman House, Bear Run, Pennsylvania, 1936. *Courtesy, Museum of Modern Art, New York*

(RIGHT) The Price Tower, Bartlesville, Oklahoma, 1956. *Courtesy, H. C. Price Company*

(OPPOSITE: TOP) Robie House, Chicago, Illinois, 1909. *Courtesy, Museum of Modern Art, New York*

(CENTER) Imperial Hotel, Tokyo, Japan, 1922. *Courtesy, Museum of Modern Art, New York*

(BOTTOM) Entrance, Johnson Wax Building, Racine, Wisconsin, 1936. *Courtesy, Johnson Wax Company*

The Solomon R. Guggenheim Museum, New York, 1959. *Helen Sweetland*

Frank Lloyd Wright at age eighty-one. *Courtesy, Los Angeles* Times

Le Corbusier, about 1950.
Courtesy, New York Times

Villa Savoye, Poissy-sur-Seine, France, 1929. *Courtesy, Museum of Modern Art, New York*

(ABOVE) Swiss Pavilion, University City, Paris, France, 1932. *Courtesy, Museum of Modern Art, New York*

(BELOW) Chapel at Ronchamp, France, 1955.

(LEFT) Chapel interior. *Courtesy, French Government Tourist Office*

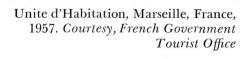

Monastery of La Tourette, Arbresle, France, 1960. *Courtesy, French Government Tourist Office*

Carpenter Center for Visual Arts, Harvard University, Cambridge, Massachusetts, 1964. *Courtesy, Harvard News Office*

Le Corbusier, with tape measure he used to explain his modulor system, 1950. *Courtesy, Wide World Photos*

new lightweight technology, however, war broke out. The war virtually paralyzed the building industry for many years. Hitler stopped Le Corbusier from entering what might have been an entirely new phase in his development.

Yet the war years were by no means a waste for the industrious Le Corbusier. If he couldn't build, he could still paint and formulate on paper more city plans, diagrams, and ideal buildings. And, most important, he could study and research a problem that had been preoccupying him since, as an awestruck youth, he'd first gazed on the amazingly proportionate Parthenon. The system of measurement that resulted—the modulor—would aid architects for generations to come and bring its inventor some of the worldwide acclaim he had always felt was his due.

A Unit For Life

Le Corbusier was working on murals in a vacation house at Cap Martin near Monte Carlo when World War II began. Erratic in so many other ways, he was highly organized and systematic in all phases of his work. "For seven years I was able to give only Saturday afternoons and Sundays to painting," he once explained. "Then, later, until the war, I was able to paint every morning from eight to one."

During the war, Le Corbusier could give plenty of time to his art; there were no building commissions on his books. And he kept painting until pigments, canvases, and even bits of plywood were exhausted.

When the Germans attacked in May 1940, Le Corbusier left

Paris for the Pyrenees. His artistic materials nearly gone, he began experimenting with reconstruction projects. He concentrated mainly on prefabricated housing and methods of dry construction. The "Murondins," which he designed in 1940, were self-built structures designed for a European population uprooted by war; all made use of very simple materials easily available or actually on the site. He also sketched schemes for "flying schools"—portable units for child refugees. If the army had movable huts, he reasoned, then why not portable classrooms?

He wrote, designed, and illustrated several more books; submitted his ill-fated master plan for Algiers to the government; and founded an Association for Designers for an Architectural Renewal. But mainly, with the world in ruins about him, Le Corbusier delved deeply into those systems of proportion used by builders of the past, such as the "golden section." All through his life he had preached the necessity of a rule or law in art, the "regulating lines." For him this rule was poetic vision; he even wrote and published a "Poem to the Right Angle."

Corbu wanted to develop a universal rule, a system of proportioning that could be used by engineer and architect alike. His dream was for every object designed for human use to correspond to a simple all-pervading harmony. This was the gift he wanted to hand down to generations to come. It took him decades of historical research, much debate and experimentation, and some very complicated mathematics (all described carefully in two books) before he finally succeeded. The result—his modulor system—is a gradually diminishing scale of proportionate dimensions based on a six-foot man with hand uplifted. It makes possible an infinite number of variations within a unit system and is applicable to the design of anything from a piazza to a bookshelf. Furthermore, it is apparently the only numerical scale that relates the foot and inch system to the metric system and vice versa.

The bulk of work on the modulor was completed during the war years, and many dedicated people helped Corbu, crossing the Savoy border to meet him. All of them took great risks to continue this collaboration during the German occupation.

The modulor system was first used in the design of the Marseilles apartment block completed after the war; a picture of the modulor man is inscribed in the building's concrete base. From then on everything Corbu designed was based on this scale, which was conceived with as much mysticism and poetic passion as mathematics. And he obviously expected everyone the world over to follow suit. When he sent the drawings for his Harvard Carpenter Arts building across the ocean to the United States, they were without a scale. When a cable pointing this out arrived in France, Le Corbusier simply replied irritably, "You have the modulor."

How did the world react to his invention? The response ran the gamut from admiration and enthusiasm to ridicule and incomprehension. Albert Einstein, shown the modulor by Corbu at Princeton, called it "a range of dimensions which makes the bad difficult and the good easy." But others scoffed at Le Corbusier's various odes to his creation and termed it obscure and paradoxical. The patent engineer who examined the numbers, figures, and diagrams told the architect, "In my life . . . this hour spent with you shall be a landmark." But a British architecture critic called the system "a ragbag of ideas presented with such seductive success for a decade that they have seemed as modern as tomorrow's Sputnik."

Corbu was nothing if not a salesman, and he had no sooner surprised the world with his concept than he was lecturing on it all over the globe: in 1947 he explained it to American architects, packing the amphitheatre of the Metropolitan Museum in New York. Soon after he spoke to Colombian architects at Bogota. In London, the sheets he pinned up to demonstrate the modulor were torn down by the students and auctioned off. The scale was the main topic of CIAM's Sixth Congress in Bridgewater, England, and of two events at Milan.

But Le Corbusier had dreamed of his system being used by every designer—mason, carpenter, industrial engineer, and joiner, as well as architect—for standardization in manufacturing. Like so many of his hopes, this was never realized. The system was widely applied only by builders.

His grandiose plans were still alive during the war, however, and work on the modulor helped to fill the hours and to keep him sane. For those six years of enforced idleness in his profession were not kind to him. He was forced to give up his Paris apartment and his studio. He was also very ill for a while. To top it all off, if the reports of French acquaintances are accurate, during the occupation Corbu's wife Yvonne suffered from malnutrition, broke her leg, and lost much of her former beauty. At any rate, the effects of all this had to be further isolation and loneliness for a man who had always had difficulty with close personal relationships.

There *were* a few extremely devoted friends through the years. But these were constantly being disowned the minute they made a mistake or betrayed the architect: his teacher L'Eplattenier, his friend and cohort Ozenfant, and most recently his cousin and close friend Charlotte Perriand. In the same way, Le Corbusier would periodically fire all his designers in one swoop, whenever they became tired, slack, old, or uncreative. He'd also attack followers who imitated him, and other architects he felt had become slack.

Still, Corbu did have many admirers. They mobbed him and applauded him and asked for his autograph wherever he traveled. Young architects from Poland, Spain, Japan, South America, England, and the United States came to his studio to work as underpaid draftsmen under his tutelage just for the privilege of saying "I once worked for Le Corbusier." (In the same way, young apprentices flocked to Wright's Taliesin.)

As Allied armies closed in upon Berlin, Corbu turned his attention to the major task confronting France both socially and architecturally—the rehousing of some four million uprooted families in France alone. Even though he was almost sixty, his vitality was amazing. Although he had recovered from his wartime illness, he was still not in the best of health, and he was nearly without economic resources.

The first postwar challenge to come his way was a request from the town officials of the historic center of Saint-Dié in eastern France. Ten thousand residents had been evacuated before the city was systematically razed by the Germans, block by block, with mines and grenades, over the course of three days and three nights. Many of Le Corbusier's designs of the 1920s and 1930s had never been built, and he could easily have reworked some of them a little to fit this particular problem. Instead, he proposed a bold, beautiful solution that startled followers who had not sensed his gradual drift toward the sensual and sculptural, the primitive and practical. His plan resulted in Saint-Dié being called the most beautiful city never built, just as his Palace for the Soviets was termed the finest building never built.

In 1945 Le Corbusier visited the site of the bombed-out Saint-Dié in the Vosges and sketched a reconstruction plan on the spot. It was revolutionary in three respects: first, it applied his formula of the housing unit (*unité d'habitation*) to a small town; second, it called for a linear industrial city of plants, warehouses, and public utility installations that was separate from the civic center but close to transportation and communication lines (highways, rivers, and railroads); and third, it created a splendid, spacious pedestrian piazza at its core. It is this last suggestion that makes the Saint-Dié plan stand out not only above other architects', but also above all Corbu's previous city diagrams.

Dynamic, yet as peaceful as any Renaissance plaza, this main area, which was on a kind of platform one thousand feet across, was approached by river-spanning ramps and bridges. It was designed for walkers—even scaled to the distance a man might cover in a quarter of an hour on foot. Citizens were meant to meander all around the various civic monuments and buildings, set like sculptural pieces in this giant paved garden.

Unfortunately, reaction to the Saint-Dié plan was not entirely favorable. Some say only one local industrialist vetoed it for economic reasons. Others say rejection came from all sides of the political spectrum—socialists, communists, and industrialists. In the end, only one of Le Corbusier's buildings rose against the landscape of Saint-Dié—a factory for young Jean-Jacques Dival, who was interested in art and ideas. The new city plan finally chosen was nothing more than an academic reproduction of the old.

As if in recompense, the architect's next reconstruction

proposition was carried through. It turned out to be the building of which he was most proud, and it was the scandal of his
career. It was actually an apartment building in Marseilles, but
it was much more than just one apartment building. It was a
way of life—and so the name L'Unité d'Habitation. It was a
genuine unit for the whole of life.

The creator of this monolith called it the child of "forty years'
gestation." It was the culmination of all his research into housing and communal living. It was a synthesis of all his utopian
ideas, for he believed great architecture should not only mirror
a manner of living but propose one.

Work on the Marseilles block began in 1945. The Germans
had blown up the port, and the housing situation for the working people of the city was critical. They had lost shelter, furnishings, clothing, even kitchen utensils. The French Minister of
Reconstruction, Eugène Claudius-Petit, invited Le Corbusier to
apply his talents, unconditionally, to rehousing the refugees.
Recognition from the government of France, his adopted country, was late, but it was finally coming.

Not that there were no problems once Corbu accepted.
Claudius-Petit had to fight many a battle against opposing authorities. And so did the architect, who wrote a number of
defensive books and pamphlets during the course of construction. Professional jealousy, political pressure, frustration,
misrepresentation—all of these abounded.

"Five years of storm, spite and uproar . . . despicable, ugly, a
hue and cry by the press," Le Corbusier wrote in retrospect.
Before it was all over, there were ten changes of government,
seven successive ministers of reconstruction, and suits and
charges of every description.

The first obstacle was haggling over the site. Plans were
delayed for three years while the Municipality of Marseilles
tried to decide among three locations, finally choosing the most
beautiful—the Boulevard Michelet. Actually this gave Le Corbusier and his team of young assistants (his orders were that
only the young could work on this project) time to think. "In a
studio parallel to my own," he said, "engineers and architects
were assembled, some clever and wily like foxes in the thicket of

technique, others devoted and impassioned like true fighters for a cause—the cause of civilization."

The architect approached the problem of Marseilles as he always approached problems—from an intellectual, rational point of view, properly stating the problem so that the correct solution would be indicated. Typically he let it gestate for several weeks, then sketched (on anything handy, often the back of an envelope) a preliminary drawing. Next came what looked like a ten-year-old's crude crayon rendering, in four colors on transparent paper, of what Corbu called the "organism." His international crew of helpers then filled in details like staircases, facades, and so on. The finished plans were finally handed to Andre Wogenscky, a talented young builder who became Le Corbusier's right-hand man after the war. Wogenscky was particularly able in handling construction crews, and at Marseilles he virtually lived on the site while the building was going up.

The structure that finally went up in 1952 was a huge slab containing three hundred and sixty apartments of twenty-three different types to house sixteen hundred people. It stands on thirty-four cyclopean legs spread wide to support fifteen hundred tons each (a gradual evolution from the slender columns under his 1920s villas). These thick legs carry an extra first floor, termed the "artificial ground level," which houses all the services: water, electricity, heat, and sewage. Above that are seventeen stories of apartments. Halfway up, two stories are given over to social activities and services—household shops, barber shop, laundry, library, post office, hotel for guests, and a splendid double-story restaurant and club with a window two hundred and fifty feet long. (The whole building is equipped with a grand total of twenty-six kinds of communal facilities.) Topping all this is Corbu's magnificent roof garden, which distinguishes the Marseilles block from all that went before. Here, one hundred and eighty feet up, is a huge plaza rimmed by a high parapet and filled with sculptural ventilation shafts; a gymnasium; great concrete tunnels and caves for children to play in; a nursery school for one hundred and fifty youngsters, complete with paddling pool, sunbathing platforms, and a row of curved concrete benches for mothers; a free-standing vertical concrete slab to serve as a screen for nighttime projection of films; a thousand-foot cinder racetrack; and a cantilevered balcony on which lovers can sit in privacy and watch the sunsets. Le Corbusier, it seemed, had thought of everything.

Visitors, especially Americans, were amazed at the building materials used by one they considered the most modern of modern architects. Instead of a smooth sleek surface composed of the engineered synthetics—aluminum, plastic, and glass—Le Corbusier chose a crude look. The exterior was of rough raw concrete, which was to become the insignia of a new movement in postwar architecture. The pebble aggregate was left exposed, as well as the imprints of the wooden molds (a man-made imprint, says critic Peter Blake, that seems a deliberate affirmation of man in a machine age).

Actually, the choice of such materials was an economic necessity. The steel with which the Unité was originally supposed to be built was too expensive and too scarce in France after the war. And the architect had been moving toward more primitive components anyway. Unfinished concrete was cheaper, and Corbu, with his deep sense of tradition and continuity, wanted finishes on his buildings that would age well rather than turn streaky and gray.

That he was delighted with the finish at Marseilles is readily seen by something he said at the structure's inauguration: "The defects shout at one from all parts: Luckily we have no money! . . . Exposed concrete shows the least incidents of the shuttering, the joints of the planks, the fibers and knots of the wood, etc. . . . In men and women do you not see the wrinkles and the birthmarks, the crooked noses, the innumerable peculiarities? . . . Faults are human; they are ourselves, our daily lives. What matters is to go further, to live, to be intense, to aim high, and to be loyal."

Such careful thought about man's nature and needs went into every aspect of the Unité's planning. This is why such authorities as Milan's Dr. Ernesto Rogers, a leading European architect, called the building "the great monument raised by Le Corbusier to man as he is . . . the first palace raised by man not to the prince, but to the ordinary man."

In a radical departure from the customary sleek facing, the block's facade is three-dimensional, protruding here and there in a grill or honeycomb effect. The apartments are slid into the slab like so many drawers into a huge filing cabinet. Each has two heavy balconies with a view of the mountains or the Mediterranean. While the general concrete surface has a natural pinkish-gray tint, the sides of the balconies are painted bright pastel colors which Corbu selected from hues he stirred around in a bowl in his studio. The sculptural variations in depth, the rhythm of light and dark rectangles, and the shimmering mosaic of balcony tints all combine to make this the most lyrical of Corbu's buildings up to that time.

The building has been likened to both an ocean liner and a monastery. An examination of the interiors of the apartments carries the comparison further. Each is laid out with the efficiency and economy of a steamer cabin. Gone are cozy nooks and corners, but there's an abundance of built-in cupboards, kitchen fittings, wardrobes, and the like. These were not only space-saving—they were necessary for a working class that had lost all its furnishings and possessions to German bombs. And, like passengers on an ocean liner, the tenants are provided with most of life's necessities almost on their doorstep (the facilities on the "indoor street" of the seventh and eighth floors). Though the sixteen hundred inhabitants are in some ways like a collective organization, the Unité—like a monastery—offers total individual privacy as well. Each apartment provides every family member with space for isolation, reading, and hobbies. And each apartment is insulated from the others with lead pads.

A staircase leads from the combination living-dining area to the master bedroom, which juts out over, like a gallery. The apartments—ranging from those for childless couples to those for families with six to eight children—are really designed as "temples to family life." The kitchen is the core, and the children's bedrooms, separated by sliding partitions, are farthest from the parents', allowing "psychological and acoustical privacy."

The double-height living rooms have fifteen-foot-high windows that provide a magnificent view, fresh air, and sunlight. The building itself is oriented so that the sun moves around it each day and every frontage gets its fair share. Balconies form a sort of sun screen.

From Corbu's point of view, the apartment block was a compromise. It should have been three times as high, and there should have been nine or ten others, each with a twelve-acre park, spreading across a landscaped terrain to the sea—Le Corbusier's city of the future. But he accepted it as a most successful demonstration of all his favorite theories and was noticeably proud. He delighted in showing a diagram illustrating the alarming acreage ordinary houses and roads would require to accommodate the same population housed in his Unité. He referred to his sculptural garden on top as a "roof and landscape worthy of Homer." He spent a whole day guiding Picasso through the building and afterward mentioned with obvious satisfaction that the painter then wanted to go to Corbu's studio "to see how one makes architectural plans." (The architect probably valued this artist's opinion above all others, for he considered himself to be the Picasso of architecture.) Usually one to hide out from the "prying press," Le Corbusier posed proudly for photographers while trotting around his rooftop track in gym attire. And for all the remaining years of his life, the photo that dominated his office wall was one of laughing children playing on his Marseilles roof.

On the bright fall evening of October 14, 1952, dignitaries from France and architects from all over the world came to celebrate the opening of this ideal community and apartment building. Noted architect Walter Gropius was one of those attending. Gazing around at the sculptural power of the Unité, he said, "Any architect who does not find this building beautiful had better lay down his pencil."

These admiring words from his former associate were particularly gratifying to Le Corbusier in the face of the furor of criticism from so many others. No less an illustrious public body than the Council of State formally reprimanded the Minister of Reconstruction for having, on Corbu's request, suspended certain building rules. The Unité itself became a political shuttlecock. The municipality reduced all subsidies as far as possible so that many of the tenants were not of the humble working class as originally intended. Maladministration of the apartment's indoor shopping street (administrators demanded that stores be bought, not rented—a risk too great for a small proprietor) kept the center empty for a long time.

Practically every charge possible has been leveled against the building: the rooms are too narrow and provide too little privacy; the corridors are bare and forbidding; the master bedroom, overlooking the living room, collects all the noise and odors emanating from below; the master bedroom is so public that undressing there is like performing on stage; the shopping center is like a ghost town because French housewives prefer shopping out on the street; children would rather play on neighboring playgrounds than on the roof garden; there are no schools (except the nursery); there is no public realm or political space as in Saint-Dié; life inside the flats is too standardized, harmonized. On learning that building costs amounted to two billion francs, one constructor commented that two comfortable and more private houses could have been built for the price of every single apartment. A tenant, on hearing that Le Corbusier was often labeled a functionalist, said, "Then he is a functionalist who does not function like the rest of us."

Replied Corbu to all such complaints, "I like the Marseillians. They yell a lot," and "Let them all bark."

Perhaps some of the criticisms are valid, but when one objective surveyor visited the Unité a few years ago, he found a plurality of urban life in the flats, each tenant having personalized his own apartment with bric-a-brac and individual possessions. He found all the stores in the shopping center occupied; though the center was not being used exclusively, it was at least providing an alternative to the hustle and bustle and perhaps inclement weather out in the street. He found children playing on the roof and wading in the pool, safe there even without supervision as they could not be on a busy thoroughfare. And he found a strong sense of communal identity. "All in all," concluded the architectural writer and historian, "the Unité is what it was intended to be—a radical alternative to suburban sprawl, where groups of sixteen hundred people form a manageable-sized association that gives the benefits of individual privacy and collective participation in one unity."

Although outsiders continued to gripe and the building remained for many years the most controversial on the continent, the residents themselves seemed to settle down and even to exhibit a certain pride in living in Le Corbusier's test tube.

The architect, in the meantime, had turned to other battles. While Unité construction was still going on, Corbu was far away in New York. Despite misgivings arising from his last visit to America, he had accepted an invitation to be French representative on a commission to select the site for the United Nations headquarters. The chance to make up for the League of Nations disappointment and to finally build a seat for a potential world government enticed him.

The site agreed upon was a seventeen-acre tract along the East River in Manhattan, a gift of John D. Rockefeller, Jr. Le Corbusier next became one of ten architects selected from all over the world to plan the United Nations building. Ensconced in an office on the twenty-first floor of the RKO building, he went eagerly to work. But for this particular architect to work as a team member was virtually impossible. As he'd done many years before in Rio, Corbu tried to take over the whole show. In the end, the job of overall administration was given to a more diplomatic American, Wallace Harrison, designer of the Rockefeller Center. In an act reminiscent of the League incident, Le Corbusier immediately accused Harrison of pirating his design and of getting his position because he was related by marriage to the Rockefeller who'd donated the United Nations site. Once again Americans were glad to say goodbye to the cantankerous French architect, whom they now considered to be a bad loser of the worst sort.

Typically, when the United Nations building was complete, Corbu penned his own addendum: "A new skyscraper which everyone calls the 'Le Corbusier building' has appeared in New York. L.C. was stripped of all his rights, without conscience and without pity." He was exaggerating, of course. Though the finished structure *was* a somewhat inferior version of his plan, no one ever considered calling it the Le Corbusier building.

The only good thing that came of this second bitter experience in the United States was the architect's friendship with New York sculptor Tino Nivola. Born in Sardinia of peasant stock, Nivola was the kind of uncomplicated, simple and sincere person Corbu felt he could trust—she was actually very much like his wife. (In fact, Nivola recalled later, "I first really began to understand Corbu when I met his wife. She was a wonderfully funny, primitive type, the only person who never really took Corbu seriously as a great figure.")

While the United Nations battle raged, the architect often retreated on evenings and weekends to the sculptor's Eighth Street studio in Greenwich Village, where he would paint furiously. Or he went out to Amagansett at the end of Long Island to Nivola's frame and clapboard house. There, wearing shorts, a bright sports shirt, and the ever-present dark-rimmed glasses, Le Corbusier took long walks along the beach, played with his friend's children, or worked on a new type of sand sculpture developed by Nivola. One weekend, to repay the sculptor's kindness, Corbu painted two huge surrealistic murals on the inside walls of Nivola's house. This was a warm, kind, and relaxed side of the public figure that few were allowed to glimpse.

Not only did Le Corbusier lose the United Nations war, but the reputation as a crotchety sorehead that he acquired from the incident resulted in his losing a UNESCO commission as well. The UNESCO headquarters was going to be built in Paris, and he was a natural to get the job. But since the United States was putting up most of the money, its state department officials had a major say in choosing an architect. They vetoed the tactless Corbu at once (ironically, the decision was made only one day before he was voted an honorary member of the National Institute of Arts and Letters in America). To make sure he didn't get the job, they appointed him to the board charged with selecting the architect, a devious but successful device. Even after three capable builders were chosen, Le Corbusier still tried to get in on the project. "It was tragic to see how bitterly hurt he was to have been denied this third opportunity to realize his League of Nations Palace," said one witness.

But his hurt and bitterness didn't interfere with his work. Usually up at six, he made his daily run before breakfast, and then went to his drawing board. He had an excellent reputation for delivering plans on time. He could usually be found either working before a huge board he'd rigged up across two chairs in his studio apartment, or at his office, where a small separate room was the scene of all his studies and interviews. Here he conducted his business efficiently, but without all the usual mechanical accoutrements. Only a typewriter and a secretary assisted him.

In the last years of the 1940s, he concentrated on more abortive city plans. As one observer commented, "His output of city plans is remarkable, not only in sheer size, but also in terms of futility. Few were commissioned, fewer still were paid for, and perhaps none stood the slightest chance of being adopted."

One scheme of this period that did stand a chance almost right up to the wire was a rather romantic project for a pilgrimage center at Sainte-Baume. Edouard Trouin, a geometrician, owned some land in the hills between Marseilles and Toulon, and it was here that Mary Magdalene had supposedly passed her last years. Impressed perhaps by the mathematics of Le Corbusier's modulor, or by the Unité then rising in Marseilles, Trouin asked the architect to design a place of forgiveness and peace. Corbu's meticulous pen-and-ink sketches called for an underground basilica, stepped clusters of hermit cells that adjusted beautifully to the steeply sloping mountainside, and a hotel for pilgrims.

Unfortunately, just as everything seemed all set, violent opposition arose to the idea of a "modern" pilgrimage center, and cries of "scandalous" were heard again in the land. Corbu was particularly aggrieved at this latest attack. The Sainte-Baume plan is practically forgotten now, but it opened up new perspectives for the architect.

The project may have led, however, to Le Corbusier's being commissioned to design a new chapel at Ronchamp two years later. And in 1949 Corbu made use of the plans for the pilgrimage center when he designed vacation housing for Cap Martin. His design called for a series of dwellings gracefully elevated and integrated with the landscape. The only one to go up, though, was a cabin that Corbu designed for himself in modulor dimensions. Far from what you'd picture a vacation home on the French Riviera to be, his was a cramped six-foot-by-fifteen-foot "shack" with a corrugated iron roof. (Poorly paid as architects go, he lived frugally, shunned entertainment, and dressed austerely.) In his cabin near Monte Carlo, the architect summered in seclusion for the last fifteen years of his life, sketching and exercising every day.

As the 1950s approached, Le Corbusier could look back on only one crowning achievement of the postwar years—the Marseilles block. And the good memories were probably crowded out by all the sad stories—the Saint-Dié plan, United Nations, UNESCO, Sainte-Baume, and the unexecuted city plans.

But the continued adulation of the young must have been a solace. Throughout his life, his greatest satisfaction came not from the praise of art critics, but from the simple comments of people who understood his buildings and what he wanted to do with them. Pointing to his studio photos of playful children on the Unité roof, he would explain that he liked the picture because it proved that architecture could make people happier. It was this conviction that appealed to youth.

Detractors called him "Pope Corbu" and his followers (some of whom even adopted the same dark-rimmed glasses) "all the little Corbus." But in young admirers' eyes he was a prophet, in a category with Einstein, Picasso, Bertrand Russell, Gandhi, and Martin Luther King, Jr. "Beyond his creative contribution," wrote Charles Jencks, "Le Corbusier gave to the modern movement a moral stature and strength which was also quite unique. Recognized as a constant fighter against certain anachronistic tendencies of the Academies, or even against unthinking modernism, he was always looked up to as an uncompromising figure of integrity and conscience."

A Chapel . . . and a City

In 1950, two projects that would be among the most significant of his career came to the sixty-five-year-old Le Corbusier. News of both arrived at his cubbyhole office the same week.

A delegation of the Indian government came to place in his lap the dream of a lifetime—a chance to finally build a city from scratch. This was to be the Punjab capital, Chandigarh, at the foot of the Himalayas. Word also came that a French archbishop and even the Pope had approved a first model for a pilgrim chapel to go up on a high hill in the Vosges. This was to be the Chapel of Notre-Dame-du-Haut de Ronchamp, often called Corbu's most remarkable and most moving work. These two great projects, plus the monumental Dominican Monastery of La Tourette, were to dominate the last seventeen years of his life.

There had been a chapel at Ronchamp for many centuries, perched atop a splendid bluff and visited by many pilgrims. But Allied artillery had destroyed it during the Second World War. All that was left was the rubble, which Le Corbusier was to use in the rebirth of the mission church. In the summer of 1950 he climbed the hill and meticulously studied the four horizons. "Give me charcoal and paper," he commanded, and he drew each of the four separately. These were to be his frame—the horizons to north, south, east and west. "It is they who commanded," he said later.

Up there on the bluff, Le Corbusier made another important

decision: "The idea crystallized: in these conditions at the top of that lonely place, here we must have one all-embracing craft, an integrated team, a 'know-how' composed of men, up there on the hill, free and masters of their craft."

And so it was. The architect had always been most comfortable with craftsmen, since his father had been one and he himself had grown up among them. Now, for the chapel, he assembled a team that he used as a remarkable tool—and (amazing for Corbu) that he actually loved. Years later, upon returning to Ronchamp, he spent a whole day darting about in his little green Fiat trying to find these simple men just to pass the time of day with them.

The foreman, his two sons, and four other strong and skillful men were all from Franche-Comté, an area known for its great craftsmen. One carved the chapel benches of gray African wood with his own hands. A craftsman in mirrors set and sealed each of the windows. A blacksmith wrought the handrails of cast iron made in nearby foundries. Le Corbusier himself enameled in vivid colors the eight panels of sheet steel compressing the huge processional door.

The chapel in its entirety almost defies description. Because it is like no other church or chapel ever designed, visitors receive a pamphlet or brochure upon arriving that asks them to be open and receptive to this unique structure. Though the proportions are strictly in accord with the modulor scale, there is not a single straight line in the building. What the architect did was take a proportional rectangular grid and distort it every which way like India rubber: the roof slopes downward, the wall slopes outward, and the floor slants away from the roof (downward toward the altar, following the slant of the ground). The roof, with its giant upturned edges, was inspired by a crab shell the architect had once picked up on Long Island—it remained next to his drawing board while he was designing Ronchamp. Light is admitted by a startling six-inch crack that runs all around the building between walls and roof, and by two dozen square openings that seem more like scattered, punched-out holes than windows. Through their panes of tinted glass can be seen trees, clouds, and even passersby. Three white towers with domed caps also throw light into three little side chapels hewn out of the thick walls. The intense red used occasionally in these chapels stands out against the whitewashed walls, the beautiful white marble of the altars, and the gray of the ceiling and external eaves. And the only adornment is a full-sized wooden cross—not on the altar as would be expected, but alongside it.

The chapel is very small, but its sweeping curves and broad eaves disguise this. "I defy a visitor," wrote the architect, "to give offhand the dimensions of different parts of the building." Uncluttered for the most part (only a few benches occupy the nave), the structure accommodates only two hundred standing. But its stark white walls and overhanging eaves serve as a dramatic backdrop for outdoor processions and ceremonies.

The simple peasant people of Ronchamp loved their chapel, more a piece of sculpture than a building. And the church of Rome made it a place of pilgrimage on fixed dates, so that it now attracts the faithful from all over the world. But others, like architect James Sterling and critic Nikolaus Pevsner, termed it an irrational structure, a retreat from the modern movement, having an "entirely visual appeal" without demanding "intellectual participation from the public."

Perhaps one reason for their unease is the mysterious aura and the elusive metaphysical quality of this building. Peter Blake said it possessed a mystery "reminiscent of the catacombs or the massive stone monasteries of the Middle Ages," and architect John Alford argued it could best be understood as a "symbolic fortress and tomb." Three weeks after visiting the site for the first time, Corbu recorded a clear impression of the chapel as it was finally built: "In one stroke the towers, the enormous roof, the sweeping wall freckled with oddly shaped windows." It was almost as if, in that one smudgy drawing, he was committing to paper a lifetime of associations, inspirations, and ideas. Perhaps this is why the chapel conveys such a multiplicity of images: an underground cavern, a nun's cowl, a winged airplane, a hooded monk or penitent, a ship's prow, a pair of praying hands. Although critics may not agree on the symbolism, they generally agree that Le Corbusier's Ronchamp sculpture is the most religiously convincing building of the twentieth century. That this agnostic, this nonconformist, should have produced the most saintly of structures is just one more paradox in the life of this most paradoxical of men. Though he scoffed at honors, he spent a lifetime grumbling about the world's rejection. Though he loathed the establishment, he was probably the only man in the world who had a Legion of Honor ribbon pinned on *both* his jacket and his outer overcoat. A rebel against every convention of his time, he was a paragon of orderliness in his work, his painting, and his physical fitness routine.

It is typical of the enigmatic Le Corbusier that, after creating the Ronchamp pilgrimage center, he should turn around and come up with the Dominican monastery of La Tourette. No two buildings could be more different, though both commissions came from the same church. The romantic, poetic chapel glories in its harmony with nature, beckoning visitors from miles away. The rigidly austere monastery dominates its landscape and repels visitors with its aloof, defensive nature. Both structures had the same advocate, however—the Parisian Dominican Père Couturier.

As at Ronchamp, Corbu visited and studied the site, which he later described as "a steeply sloping valley, wreathed with woods and opening out onto a plain." And again he sketched the far horizons. Though it took him three years this time to prepare the plans and models, it is said that none of his other buildings caused him so little vexation. Perhaps this was because he was so sure of what he wanted to do. Ever since his visit, as a traveling student, to the Carthusian monastery of Ema, he had retained his fascination with monasticism and the relationship between the private and the collective. Now, in this monastery of his own, completed in 1960, he produced his most nearly perfect communal building—perfect both visually and functionally. Apart from having to fit into a steep and difficult (but wholly commanding) site, the structure's shape and plan were left entirely to the architect. As one friar said, "Le Corbusier knows what we are and what we want." And, having actually lived most of his life as a monk, the architect did.

The result was the closest he ever came to realizing his long-envisioned ideal of reconciling the individual and the group. Teetering on the side of a rugged hill, the monastery has the closed, almost violent appearance of a fortress. Horizontal layers containing an open-roof cloister, monks' cells, class-rooms, a library, and a refectory spill down the slope. The upper part—two floors of just over one hundred cells—extends over the lower. These rugged and solid floors contrast effec-tively with the tall windows of undulating glass in the common room and in the refectory underneath. The windows are virtu-ally a system of large vertical glass louvers. A staccato pattern of black holes is created by the private balconies fronting each cell. These individual rooms, like the apartments at Marseilles, all receive sunlight for some part of the day. And like the build-ing's kitchens, laundry, stores and so on, all are clean and light and well equipped.

Le Corbusier had always concerned himself with both inter-nal and external traffic ways. At La Tourette he made a very clear distinction between places of individual retreat and places of collective celebration—"of contacts and circuits."

If you were to visit the monastery today, the monks would guide you down the long empty corridors (bare except for essential radiators, doors, and brightly painted water pipes). They would point out the sudden unexpected glimpses of na-ture, the changes in light, and the way all forms move in relationship. They haven't been specially trained as guides. They're simply responding as the architect himself would. At last Le Corbusier had found his ideal tenants, men who knew how to appreciate and live fully within the Spartan environ-ment.

In the single chamber of the monastery's great church, he created one of his most memorable structures. The chamber, which is two hundred feet long and fifty feet high, includes the sacristy, the chapel of the Blessed Sacrament, and the lower church. Like the sides of a box, the rough concrete walls rise "unimpeded, uncarved and unbroken from floor to ceiling on all four sides." Instead of windows there are horizontal slits of unequal widths near the floor, and, as at Ronchamp, a strip of light all around between walls and ceiling. The whole impression is one of stark, brutal forms in tight relation. The only piece of modeling or carving in the whole monastery is a small crucifix on the altar of the Blessed Sacrament. Every line of the La Tourette building defines to precision the life of the monastic—exclusion of the world, repudiation of wealth, quiet study and meditation, aloofness, simplicity, and harmony.

The reason Le Corbusier, who was not religious in any usual sense, was able to give this monastic definition such accuracy was that he took the measure of the men he built for as nearly exactly and universally as possible. Like Ronchamp, La Tourette was for him "a program on the human scale." He never built for princes or supermen, for communists or capitalists. Architecture was never anything purely political, social, or even religious. As he'd written twenty years earlier, "Architecture needs a human idiom."

With the waning of the 1950s, Le Corbusier, nearing seventy, was still crowding as much into the working day as possible. Several other Unités were on the drawing board. In Ahmedabad, the center of India's cotton spinning area, a number of his designs were being realized—a museum, several villas, and a building for the Millowners' Association. The latter contained a sweepingly curved assembly hall. And a quarter century after the construction of his Swiss Pavilion, he and Lucio Costa were building the Brazilian dormitory in the same Cité Universitaire.

After the dormitory was completed, Le Corbusier told a friend, "People are going to say I contradict myself; that after building Ronchamp and having many exclaim, 'Thank God that Le Corbusier got rid of his box architecture,' I am going back to building boxes in the Brazilian Pavilion in the University City of Paris.

"This is because they do not understand that I am mainly concerned with the different nature of the problems I have to solve," he explained, "and Ronchamp could not be a series of boxes, while by nature other buildings are."

As if to show this flexibility and easy adaptability to different problems, Corbu, within the span of a decade, produced two extreme contrasts—on one hand the Jaoul house at Neuillysur-Seine (in the peasant, primitive vein of building), and on the other the Phillips Pavilion in Brussels and the Centre Le Corbusier in Zurich (both in modern, mathematical vein).

When Le Corbusier was asked to design the Phillips Pavilion at the Brussels World's Fair in 1958, however, he chose to propagandize the "lyricism of modern life." He had become interested in the modulations and subtle inflections of music, and he translated the concept into architecture. But at Brussels he wanted to concentrate more on the message than on the medium, more on the content than on the form. So, after he formulated sketches and models for the pavilion facade—sort of a series of tightly knit, sloping tents or shells cast in sand molds on the ground—the details were turned over to composer-engineer Xenakis. Corbu spent his time combining existing sensory technologies into a new form of light and sound show, a forerunner of the electronic-media environments Marshall McLuhan was later to analyze.

Spectators were bombarded with all sorts of projected images—some terrifying, others peaceful and harmonious. The architect collected the art for the show himself from various museums. And music—or, rather, the three-dimensional sound arrangement conceived by Edgar Varese and Xenakis—was distributed around the interior shell by four hundred amplifiers.

Le Corbusier's last exhibition center—his final building—was another odd, modernistic structure; "his most convincing essay in lightweight technology," it has been called. It was constructed of thin steel, glass, and crisp panels enameled in the architect's clearest collection of colors, with all right-angled corners and not a single curved wall or screen. Its gray steel roof, which hovers independently, resembles two sheet-metal parasols. The most apt description of this Le Corbusier center beside a lake in Zurich is that it resembles "a beached ship." Under the battleship-gray ceiling are metal doors with semicircular openings like hatches, steel ladders and periscope holes which push through the "top deck," and a double-height exhibition center whose metal decking and funnel are reminiscent of a vessel's boiler room. The whole pavilion is "pure, neat, clear,

clean and healthy," as the architect envisioned ocean liners to
be.

That Le Corbusier could have produced, so late in life, such a
different alternative to his brute forms is testimony to his creative acuity and his ability to respond to new situations.

What detractors for the most part failed to take into account
was the richness and wealth of detail Corbu would consider in
designing or executing a project. A scheme for a hospital in
Venice that he was working on when he died, for example,
contained many of the elements that city-planning theorists had
found missing from his earlier urban plans. In his last years,
which fortunately were his busiest and most inventive, Le Corbusier revealed in one work after another his complete mastery
over every variety of form. There was landscaping for a dam in
the Himalayas; a project for a French embassy in Brasilia; and
designs for an art museum in Stockholm and for churches in
South America and in Firminy, France. There was also a youth
and cultural center for Firminy, an inclined linear building one
side of which was to shield a stadium for ten thousand people
(the stadium was completed after Corbu's death). And at long
last there was a building in the United States—the fifteen-
hundred-thousand-dollar Carpenter Arts Center at Harvard,
whose construction he directed from long distance and which
he never saw. It fits well into a narrow, traditional site and
possesses, says one dean, not only amazing functional efficiency
but a "soul-satisfying greatness that is too rare in architecture."
From the drawing board, too, came schemes for a Congress
Hall in Strasbourg, an electronic calculator center for Olivetti at
Rho-Milan, an unusual international art center for a site in the
open country of Erienbach-Frankfurt, and a monumental
stadium for Baghdad.

And side by side with all these projects, of course, there was
Chandigarh, Corbu's built-from-scratch city, which he worked
on from 1951 until his sudden death in 1965. When the two
Punjabi delegates appeared in Le Corbusier's studio around
Christmas of 1950 to talk about their new capital city, it was out
of necessity. A master plan for the town had already been
designed by the New York firm of Mayer, Whittlesey and Glass,

but Matthew Nowicki, the brilliant young Polish architect who was supposed to implement the plan, had died in a plane crash in August. The delegation was forced to seek a replacement. A visit to Rome had proved futile, and in Paris, Perret was rejected as "too classical." That was why the delegates ended up on Corbu's doorstep.

They offered to engage him as architect at four thousand pounds a year on the condition that he move to India for three years to work on the site. The salary was ridiculously low, and Le Corbusier, from past experience, probably never expected the city to materialize anyway. But he didn't refuse point-blank. Instead he bought the two delegates tickets to Marseilles so they could inspect his Unité d'Habitation. The sight was overwhelming. Indians were unaccustomed to high-rises; in fact, most still slept on the floor or on the roof and refused even to board an elevator. When the Punjabi emissaries returned to Corbu's studio, they told the architect that one condition of his contract must be no high-rise buildings in Chandigarh.

The desire to finally construct his own city had, by this time, triumphed over all of Corbu's misgivings. He agreed to head a team that would include Maxwell Fry and Jane Drew, pioneers of modern architecture in England and West Africa, and his cousin and longtime associate Pierre Jeanneret. In February 1951 Le Corbusier viewed for the first time the windswept plain at the foot of the Himalayas where Chandigarh was to rise. He spent one week on the site and then was ready to begin. "You can rely on us to produce the solution to the problem," he promised grandly.

After stumbling over government officials throughout most of his career, Corbu finally found in India the free hand and warm, obliging patronage he'd long been seeking. Prime Minister Nehru said, "Let this be a new town, symbolic of the freedom of India, unfettered by the tradition of the past . . . an expression of the nation's faith in the future." He took a great interest in the project from its inception and became a personal friend of Le Corbusier.

This wholehearted backing was virtually the only advantage the architect was to enjoy, however. He found himself in an unfamiliar environment, compelled to work under unfavorable conditions. There was a complete lack of trained technicians and no means for large-scale mechanized transport; steel was in short supply, and technical services were inadequate. And both the climate and the semirural way of life ruled out his usual apartment housing.

After a lifetime of trying to master the demands of a machine age, the architect was finally building a city in an environment still largely untouched by industrialization. He began with nothing more than half a dozen concrete mixers and one crane. Recalled Maxwell Fry later, "We had twenty thousand women and children, oxen and donkeys by the thousands. We got the big concrete structure [the Palace of Justice] up with a mess of cockeyed scaffolding. We really built it like the Pyramids."

Initially Le Corbusier had been hired primarily to develop the Mayer firm's master plan. But, as usual, he soon became the dominant figure. Just a few picturesque garden-city, low-density elements of the original scheme were retained. And Corbu had soon begun redesigning the urban center to accord with his modulor, straightening major streets and reshaping slightly irregular superblocks into rectangles. Some traffic separation scheme had always been part of his city plans, and for Chandigarh he designed "the seven V's"—a division of traffic into a series of seven categories to be taken care of by a circulation system ranging from arterial roads to building corridors.

Le Corbusier at first sought to redefine the city's master plan on a suitably monumental scale, but as time went on he tended to dissociate himself from this overall designing. Instead he concentrated on the major capital complex. In all, at least eight architects were responsible for various buildings within Corbu's plan. Most of the housing—thirteen different categories—was devised by Fry and Drew, who returned to London after three years, and by Jeanneret, who remained on the site, building not only housing but also schools, clinics, and hospitals.

To the northeast of the city, Le Corbusier planned the four main buildings of his capital complex: the Secretariat, the Palace of Justice, the Assembly, and the Governor's Palace (never built). These monumental structures, interspersed with artificial hills, wide boulevards, courts, terraces, and reflecting pools, have become as much a part of every traveler's itinerary as the Taj Mahal.

Lovely scale models of the complex were carved from solid blocks of walnut by turbaned and heavily bearded Indian craftsmen. The Palace of Justice, the best known of the buildings, is tall, vaulted, and topped by a parasol roof with huge sweeping eaves. The bright pastel colors behind the irregular grille of sunbreakers contrast brilliantly with the rough concrete of the exterior. Tapestries in an abstract pattern designed by Corbu himself muffle outside sounds and take care of acoustics admirably. The Secretariat is a single eight-hundred-foot-long slab block whose monotony is broken by variations in the sunbreak pattern as well as by projections, recesses, and stair towers. A massive three-story portico with a tilted canopy fronts the square-shaped assembly hall, whose roof line is pierced from within by sculptural forms.

Even though others filled in the substance, Chandigarh, as it now stands, can be directly attributed to Le Corbusier—his only realized city scheme.

Thanks in part to the triumphs of the 1950s and 1960s—Ronchamp, La Tourette, and Chandigarh—the architect was finally getting world acclaim. Though he had built only one thing in England—an exhibition house way back in 1938—he received the Royal Gold Medal of Architecture from the Institute of British Architects in 1953. On February 4, 1960, when he lectured at the Sorbonne in Paris, forty-five hundred people thronged in front of it and fifteen hundred filled the streets outside because only three thousand could squeeze into the large amphitheatre itself. And in May 1961 the architect spent three days in the United States picking up the Gold Medal of the American Institute of Architects and a Doctor of Humane Letters degree from Columbia University. There were exhibitions of his work in France, Switzerland, and Germany, and everywhere Le Corbusier put in a personal appearance, crowds of young people jostled to get his signature on copies of his books, tried to shake his hand, and applauded him. The architect must have enjoyed these occasions, but his cantankerous nature was still evident in the crooked, slightly sarcastic smile on his thin face, and in his blasts at the establishment which were always quoted in the papers of whatever city he was visiting.

He flew into a rage when he discovered that the British architects' medal had been engraved with his legal name of Charles-Edouard Jeanneret instead of Le Corbusier. He spent his entire address before the group recounting one bitter failure after the other, referring to himself as a "true cab-horse who had received many a blow with a whip." And he would accept the American Institute's medal and Columbia's degree only on one condition: "No press, no TV, no tuxedo."

Perhaps his disposition can be ascribed to the bitter-sweet dualism that always seemed to characterize his life. There were always sad events and disappointments to shadow his greatest triumphs, even in his last years. In the autumn of 1957 his wife died. Though he kept such grief personal, it was a great blow. His longtime friend Walter Gropius says that when he met Corbu in Baghdad soon after Yvonne's death, he found him in tears and on the verge of a nervous breakdown.

There were attacks on even his greatest works up until the end. His plans for Unités at Nantes-Rezé, Meaux, Briey-en-Forêt, and Berlin were all altered because of shortages of money, losing all the freshness and brilliance of the one at Marseilles.

For his Centre Le Corbusier in Zurich, a client, Heidi Weber, had to fight city planning officials and local engineers, who called the building unsafe, and even, said Corbu, "so-called Zurich Le Corbusier friends who have harmed my activities during the realization of this Centre by uttering envious calumnies." In 1971 Heidi Weber threatened to unbolt the flexible center and rebuild it elsewhere, for the town council of Zurich wouldn't finance any exhibitions in it. They wanted it, at its original cost, only as a tourist monument. Corbu had this building constructed with twenty thousand screws so that it could, if necessary, be dismantled—probably because he realized how susceptible his earlier stationary buildings were to destruction or marring. The Weekend House he'd built outside

Paris, for example, had been demolished. His Marseilles block had vanished behind huge towers, losing its wide view of sea and mountains. The Villa Savoye, after the German occupation, was empty and decaying—it was saved from complete destruction only by the intervention of the French Minister of Culture.

Le Corbusier was even disappointed in Chandigarh, which suffered from certain formal and functional mistakes, probably because of his long absences from the site. He later told Nehru that Indian architecture in the future should gather more from its own culture, climate, and materials than from Western sources.

Less than two months before his death, four more of his city plans were rejected. No wonder he told an English reporter in his office at the time, "I see no hope."

At the age of seventy-eight he died as he had lived—alone. He had been swimming in the Mediterranean. At his funeral, the French Minister of Culture, André Malraux, told the crowd of four thousand (including ambassadors and other dignitaries) that no one "had ever been so long, so patiently insulted." The French people, and representatives from every country where Corbu had built, attempted to make up for this with a spectacular funeral ceremony. There was a torchlight procession, a military band playing marches, and an honor guard in dress uniform stationed at the bier, where thousands filed past to pay their respects.

But it's probable that Le Corbusier wouldn't have been overly impressed with this long overdue homage. It was from the joy simple men found in his buildings that he derived his deepest and most lasting satisfaction: "But suddenly you touch my hand. You do me good and I am happy and you say 'this is beautiful.' That is architecture."

Mies van der Rohe

Less Is More

Mies van der Rohe

Less Is More

Roots of Traditionalism

In the late 1880s on a construction site in Aachen, Germany, an errand boy not yet in his teens waited patiently. Then an order rang out from one of the carpenters framing the roof: "Ludwig, water!" Quickly the boy ran to a nearby lean-to and returned with the boiling water used by the builders to make coffee. He nearly stumbled in his haste, for the men would throw a sharp-edged ax or other cutting tool at him when they thought he moved too slowly.

For this humiliating fetch-it work, the boy earned a few pennies spending money. But he didn't mind the meager salary. It gave him the chance to learn about building firsthand. So did helping his father, a master mason, in his small stone-cutting shop. Though he was never to receive any formal architectural training, these first tasks were initial steps on the path to professionalism.

That youngster, Ludwig Mies, would later leave the stamp of his art and philosophy on architecture all over the world. First in his native Germany and then in his adopted country, the United States, Mies (he added his mother's surname van der Rohe when he was in his twenties) built spare, elegant towers of steel and glass that gave the modern age its characteristic look and style. Today, offspring of his buildings line important streets in every major city.

Yet he never sought fame. "It is bad to be too famous," he once remarked. "Greek temples, Roman basilicas, and medieval

113

cathedrals are significant to us as creations of a whole epoch rather than as works of individual architects. Who asks for the names of these builders?"

Perhaps it was his humble beginning as builders' runner and son of an impoverished mason that made Mies the modest, self-effacing individual he was. Unlike other architectural greats, he always tried to maintain a low profile and never felt compelled to win disciples, engage in battles, or tear down fellow architects. Once, when asked by an interviewer why he didn't construct something different for a change, he replied, "I don't want to be interesting. I want to be good."

In his entire lifetime he published only fourteen short articles. When others chose to describe their entries in the 1927 housing exhibition at Stuttgart, Germany, with pages upon pages of prose, Mies did the job in twelve concise lines entitled "About My Block."

He spoke almost as little as he wrote. Reporters had to goad him into saying anything about himself. And making public speeches before the many groups that honored him in maturity remained a painful ordeal. Normally shy and reserved, he would open up only among friends and usually only late at night, smiling a toothy grin and speaking in a slow, hesitant voice still thick with German accent.

His buildings were stark and bare, as precise and scrupulous as the maxim for which he became most widely known: "Less is more." Yet in his personal life and dress he was fussy almost to the point of dandyism. His five-foot-ten-inch frame, stocky from a taste for gourmet foods and fine wines, appeared almost slim, thanks to his elegant handstitched suits tailored in slenderizing, conservative hues. A soft, expensive handkerchief always peeked over the edge of his breast pocket. And he chainsmoked large hand-rolled cigars, a dozen or two a day.

Those who came to know him well came to understand his great and gentle nobility. In many ways he was the kindest and most gracious of men. When architect Walter McQuade was in his twenties, he spent an evening drinking gin with Mies in his quiet old Chicago apartment. He remembers this giant of modern architecture as a "marvelous raconteur," eloquent in stories and reminiscences—and in stillnesses, too.

Noted architect-writer Peter Blake likes to tell about the time he was absolutely floored by Mies's "simple, unaffected niceness." Twenty-six and fresh out of the army, Blake went to van der Rohe's apartment at nine o'clock one night, shaking in his boots. He wanted to see Mies about enrolling in his school, but mutual friends had warned, "He's very hard to meet. . . . He's very busy. . . . He's very distant. . . . It's a great imposition on him. . . ." But suddenly there was Mies, extending his hand and apologizing for not having asked young Blake to dinner. The two talked until three in the morning.

Those people who were put off by van der Rohe were in awe of the massive bulk of the architect, the lined and chiseled face, the elegant, patrician appearance, the autocratic name, and his merciless, exacting standards of craftsmanship. When one of his architectural students asked how she was to achieve self-expression in his class, he handed her a piece of paper and told her to write her name. When she had done so, he said, "Good. So much for self-expression. Now let's get down to work." When pupils submitted their sketches to him for appraisal, he often sat Buddha-like and puffed through a whole cigar before issuing his critical comments. And once, when asked his opinion of a job superintendent, he answered unequivocally, "Terrible." The man wrote letters, Mies explained, when he should have been working.

He demanded of himself the same fine workmanship he expected of pupils and employees. His high standards were a reflection of his early cultural surroundings and upbringing.

Mies was born on March 27, 1886, in the ancient city of Aachen on the border of Germany and the Low Countries. Aachen, the first capital of the Holy Roman Empire, had been the center of Western culture during the early Middle Ages. And the cathedral school which Mies attended until age thirteen had been founded by Charlemagne in the ninth century.

Even at an early age Mies was influenced by this cultural heritage. In between childish games, he stopped to admire the many ancient buildings around him. Mies was born a Roman Catholic. When he was young, he would often visit the old chapel of Charlemagne with his mother; to pass the time, he would count the stones and trace the joints. His ideals of honesty, logic, and truth were based on the moral codes of St. Augustine and St. Thomas Aquinas, whose writings Mies read and admired from youth. (In one of his rare speeches, a talk at the Illinois Institute of Technology in 1938, he told the audience, "Nothing can express the aim and meaning of our work better than the profound words of St. Augustine, 'Beauty is the splendor of truth.'")

Ideas of order and value also came from his father, who gave the boy a better knowledge of building materials than many school-trained architects possess. Learning to lay stone upon stone with skill and artistry gave the youngster a feeling for the particular heft and quality of pure materials. Later, as a practicing architect, he would go to the kiln and personally choose the bricks for his construction. "Now a brick, that's really *something*," he often remarked to associates. "That's really building. Not paper architecture . . ."

After he was graduated from elementary school, Mies attended a trade school for two years; in his spare time, he worked on various buildings his father and his father's friends were putting up around Aachen. At fifteen he left the trade school and became apprentice to several local designers and architects.

"One of my first major assignments," he remembered with amusement, "was to make drawings of neoclassical ornaments later to be rendered in stucco on the fronts of various buildings. Full-size details of Louis XIV in the morning, Renaissance in the afternoon."

So far Mies had gained all his construction knowledge on actual building sites in the rough and tumble school of dirt, noise and muscle strain. ("All education," he was fond of saying, "must begin with the practical side of life . . . the road of discipline from materials, through function, to creative work.") But until his ornamental-drawing assignment, he'd never set pen to paper. Now he was to get his first real training in draftsmanship.

"We had to draw those things on huge sheets of paper pinned on a wall," he said. "No drawing boards for us: we had to stand up, and draw this stuff swinging our arms in a big arc, covering the entire sheet with volutes and other decorative nonsense."

His disdain for such "nonsense" grew alongside a lasting love for honest materials. Nineteen-year-old Mies was happy, therefore, to leave his Aachen job in 1905 and head for Berlin. But the grueling drawing experience had developed a talent that was later to enable him to produce some of the most beautiful architectural sketches of the century.

In Berlin he worked briefly for an architect who designed mainly in wood. When Mies discovered how little he knew about that material, he decided to learn from an expert. Leading decorator and furniture designer Bruno Paul allowed the young man to work in his studio for two years. Leisure hours he filled with the reading of philosophy, sociology and natural science.

Then, in 1907, he got his first commission as an independent architect—to build a house for a Professor Riehl in a suburb of Berlin. Mies was only twenty-one. Executed in the then-popular traditional style—steep roofs, gables and dormer windows—the structure was, nevertheless, distinguishable by its precision and careful attention to detail.

"The work is so faultless that no one would guess that it was the first work of a young architect," commented one critic.

But Mies himself was not satisfied. His next stop was the office of progressive architect and industrial designer Peter Behrens, whose studio was also an early training ground for Le Corbusier and Walter Gropius. During his three years as draftsman in the studio, Mies learned greater appreciation for order and fine detail, as well as new ideas on proportion, simplicity, and the use of steel and glass. This was the influence of Behrens's industrialized building—his factories and exhibition structures.

But Behrens also had a neoclassical side to his domestic architecture that he had derived from Karl Friedrich Schinkel, a distinguished architect of Europe's romantic period. It was characterized by a unique sense of rhythm and proportion, a purity of form, and a nobility that stemmed from the practice of placing structures on wide platforms or pedestals. Mies absorbed this aspect of his tutor's work, too. In fact, a house that Mies built in 1911, at the age of twenty-five, was so romantic in spirit that it might have been done by Behrens or Schinkel.

The first suggestion of Mies's independent creative ability emerged at The Hague in Holland. The young architect went there in 1912 to confer with one of Behrens's clients, a Madame H. E. L. J. Kroller. She wanted a sumptuous home built to house her famous collection of modern paintings. A mock-up of Behrens's design had already been finished: a compact but heavy-looking two-story vertical structure. But, impressed with Mies's ability, Madame Kroller asked him to submit his own ideas in model form. His version, though still quite neoclassical in detail, was a low-slung, extended complex with a more horizontal sweep.

As it turned out, the client decided against building anything. But Mies never considered his year at The Hague wasted. (He always maintained that time is one of the cheapest commodities an architect can spend in designing a building.) For one thing, it gave him his first opportunity to advance beyond his teacher Behrens. For another, he was able to study the buildings of the Dutchman Hendrick Petrus Berlage. They strengthened his resolve always to include in his own structures the simplicity and the integrity in use of materials that characterized Berlage's work.

In 1913 the architect returned to his own office in Berlin, which he'd opened shortly before World War I began. He designed two versions of a home for himself, and commissions for several villas came in. All were classical in form, but in their simple serenity, their greater use of glass, their finer proportion and simpler detail they stood apart from—and above—their contemporaries.

At this time Mies was beginning to criticize Behrens's interest in form simply for form's sake, and to lean more toward the idea that structure is the great underlying discipline.

War interrupted his work. Because he was not a university graduate, there was no officer's commission for van der Rohe.

He served as an enlisted man in the engineer corps, building roads and bridges in the Balkans.

After returning from military service to Berlin in 1919, Mies designed a house for a Kempner family that was to be the last of his romantic works. It had a flat roof, a triple arcade, and tall narrow windows widely spaced. In that same year he began the first of five radically different and innovative projects. It was as though an Aladdin's lamp had been rubbed and the refined traditionalist Mies had been whisked away, to be replaced by a radical innovator.

A Growing Reputation

The changes in Mies van der Rohe's architecture in the first years after World War I reflected the political and artistic upheavals underway at the time. During the fighting, all artistic development had been suspended in Germany. Berlin, isolated from foreign events and influences, had existed in an artistic and intellectual vacuum. After the armistice, the liberated city seemed intent on sucking in every new movement possible. Any radical point of view in art or politics could be certain of receiving at least a hearing in postwar Germany.

Everywhere there was admiration for the new technology of the machine. Young artists like Mies (he was barely over thirty) were eager to throw off the bonds of tradition and embrace any means of expressing this new world. It was in this exhilarating atmosphere that van der Rohe dared to make a clean, absolute break with the past. His own revolution first took shape in the form of a charcoal sketch of a glass office building for Berlin. This drawing, done in 1919 for a competition, depicted a twenty-story all-glass tower, soaring like a sheer cliff of crystal. Its odd prismatic shape, angular and jagged, came not from any preoccupation with abstract or expressionist forms, but from a study of light reflections.

The same study went into Mies's second set of sketches for another all-glass skyscraper, this time thirty stories high, that he produced the following year. In fact, he even hung a model outside his office window and observed the play of light upon it. Its extraordinary free-form curves of glass provided a facade that reflected itself.

Both models were examples of his "skin and bones" architecture: a steel skeleton on the inside, a skin of glass on the outside. Both were clear, uncompromising statements of what the new technology could produce. No other architect had yet conceived of such a radical all-glass structure.

With these projects—though they were never executed—van der Rohe was catapulted into the forefront of the modern movement. The towers became the prototype of glass and metal high-rises all over the world. Ironically, the "Miesian style" became fact long before the originator finally constructed his own office skyscraper—the Seagram building in Manhattan. Forty years would pass before he got that chance.

Mies next did a study for an office building in reinforced concrete and glass. The floors were cantilevered slabs turned up and around at the edges. The niches formed around the periphery of the building were used ingeniously as storage cabinets, leaving the interior uncluttered and adaptable to any layout of offices. Here the architect used the now-common ribbon windows—an uninterrupted horizontal bank of windows—with more courage and purity than anyone preceding him. Another interesting element was the gradual tapering of the structure outward as it rose. The entrance was bare of ornamentation. Mies described this plan with characteristic succinctness: "The office building is a house of work, of organization, of clarity, of economy. . . . Maximum effort with minimum means . . . no gingerbread . . . no fortress."

Though seemingly a simple, straightforward kind of structure, this concrete office building possessed, underneath, a host of studied refinements as unobtrusive as the fine stitching on one of the architect's well-tailored suits. To Mies, "God is in the details."

A design produced in 1923 employed the material traditional in western Germany and the Lowlands—the simple brick. His brick country house is a dynamic, sculptural composition that takes advantage of all the power in the material. In his definition of the function of the wall, the architect was remarkably original. His long, independent walls didn't form a closed volume or enclose space in the ordinary sense. Instead, they directed space in a continuous pattern, so that indoors and outdoors were not clearly defined.

A milestone in the progress of modern architecture, this house, formed entirely of planes and freely flowing space, went a step beyond Wright's open plan. It was Mies van der Rohe's first announcement of a goal he would seek all his life: an architecture of space. It was also his first proposal of a freestanding wall. He later told a group of students that after this idea first occurred to him, he lay awake all night pondering whether it was legitimate. He decided it was.

For his new concept of space continuity, Mies is often said to owe something to a contemporary—Theo van Doesburg, an architect and painter who was then heading a radical renewal in the field of art. But van der Rohe said, "That is absolute nonsense. There is no influence." He resented van Doesburg's labeling him "an anatomical architect" after viewing Mies's "skin and bones" office building sketches. The painter reproached the architect for his severity. Mies was just as annoyed with van Doesburg's interlocking cubes—he accused van Doesburg of proposing the ridiculous dictum that everything should be square. The feud was one of the few van der Rohe was to get embroiled in during his lifetime.

The last of the five significant projects the architect produced in his mid-thirties was a study of mass. Reinforced concrete was used for a country house in which Mies offered completely different means of breaking up the box. It was the first of the zoned houses, eventually used successfully and extensively in the United States by architects like Marcel Breuer. A pinwheel plan was used to segregate the house's different elements—sleeping, living, and service areas—into different zones. Though never built, this concrete villa was the predecessor of the ranch house popularized so widely on the California coast by men such as Richard Neutra.

Each of Mies's five designs was a statement of principles, a generalization of a building problem, an education in itself. He probably never expected any to leave the drawing board, but, like Wright, Gropius and Le Corbusier, he was always ready to do a study at the drop of a hat. He felt that this was good training. "Make a project a year," he urged his students later when he began teaching. But usually the admonition fell on deaf ears.

Most of the architects in postwar Germany were in the same fix as young Mies—reduced to producing projects that were widely publicized, exhibited, described, and then discarded. The economic and political uncertainties of the period made architecture an unprofitable profession. Avant-gardists greatly admired Mies's pioneer sketches for their dazzling clarity and precision, but he was still regarded more as a visionary than as a practical builder. Clients never came to his door. By the end of 1924 he had not executed a single important modern building. Complimented by a friend on his building, the thirty-eight-year-old Mies observed wryly, "I have built nothing except a reputation."

But he was not idle. He wrote articles for G magazine (named for the initial letter of the German word Gestaltung, meaning "creative force"), and he financed its early issues. He organized exhibitions. He founded the Zehner Ring, a group formed to offset official prejudice against the modern movement. And mainly he worked with the Novembergruppe, an organization named after the month of the 1918 Republican Revolution and founded to improve attitudes toward modern art. From 1921 to 1925 Mies headed this group's architectural divisions and, under its banner, publicized some of his plans. He also entered a competition for the remodeling of the Alexanderplatz in Berlin. In his design he anticipated the modern office rectangle, which wouldn't become common until twenty years later.

Finally the publicity began to pay off, and the architect had chances to prove that his designs were not only buildable but practical and timeless. He built several elegant villas for wealthy businessmen in the fashionable suburbs of Berlin and the Rhineland. All were marked by precision of detail, large and simple areas of glass, bold concrete roof cantilevers, and open interior space. Like Wright's structures, all seemed at one with their sites, but, unlike Wright, Mies used classical means to achieve this: terraces, retaining walls, and short monumental flights of steps.

Modern building materials were simply not available in Germany, so Mies used brick. And he used it honestly, refusing to cover it with stucco. With his usual meticulous attention to material and detail, he calculated all dimensions in brick lengths to assure evenness at the corners. He often appeared at the kiln to choose his own bricks, sometimes separating the overfired ones from the underfired ones, using the long in one dimension and the short in the other.

Though none of his brick compositions possessed the daring of his steel and glass tower sketches, they—together with his leadership of two progressive organizations—won Mies such renown that in 1926 he was appointed first vice-president of the Deutsche Werkbund. This was an organization founded in 1907 by leading artists, architects and industrialists in order to upgrade the quality of German product design. By 1926 it had become the most powerful European proponent of quality in modern design, and was about to hold its second major exhibition at Stuttgart. Mies was named director of the effort.

If Wright or Le Corbusier had been in charge of the 1927 Werkbund exhibition at Stuttgart, chances are it would have been mainly a one-man show. But self-effacing Mies laid down the most liberal of ground rules. First, the exhibition was open to every modern European architect of any note. And second, each had much leeway in his entry.

"I have refrained from laying down a rigid program," explained the director, "in order to leave each individual as free as possible to carry out his ideas. In drawing up the general plan, I felt it important to avoid regulations that might interfere with free expression."

Unfortunately, Mies's own free expression immediately encountered opposition from officials of the city of Stuttgart. His original "general plan"—his first venture into city planning—was quite advanced and prophetic. In this unified community, the houses were arranged unevenly in blocks and steps on terraces following the natural curves of the site. Pedestrian streets, which were closed to traffic, led into many open or partially walled squares. Parking facilities were provided along the perimeter. But all this implied central ownership and control of the whole area, and the city wanted to sell the buildings separately after the exhibition. So Mies very agreeably produced a more conventional scheme, with free-standing buildings, through streets, and individual parking places for each residential unit.

The list of participants in the exhibit reads now like a Who's Who of famous modern builders of that time: Le Corbusier, Gropius, Behrens, J. J. P. Oud, Victor Bourgeau, Bruno Taut, and Hans Poelzig. These men produced thirty-three living complexes—both single-family dwellings and apartment blocks—that were models of the advanced spirit. All were white except for one red building, and all were tied together and related to the horizon by the apartment building Mies himself designed.

Mies's building was a beautiful, steel-framed structure with long bands of glass and a sheltered roof garden. But it was the interiors of the apartments that were most interesting. The simple skeleton system, with only kitchen, stairway, and toilet fixed, provided all sorts of flexibility. Through rearranging storage walls and movable partitions, twelve different units could be formed. And the installations within were a milestone in modern furniture design; they were the first of a number of pieces Mies was to produce in collaboration with a brilliant partner, Lilly Reich. Every object was impeccably crafted and calculated down to the last millimeter. With studied exactness each was placed for best effect and relation to the architectural elements. Mies turned the display of objects and the placing of things in space into an art. Furniture was positioned to direct the flow of traffic. Chairs, couches and tables were almost always free-standing, to emphasize the spatial character of a room. There were no cozy retreats or nooks where residents could derive comfort from sitting with their backs against a wall—he only allowed a bed to be against the wall.

Also exhibited at the Stuttgart apartments was the architect's most famous chair—the MR. This elegant tubular cantilevered chair with semicircular supports was an immediate success. Others were developing similar pieces simultaneously, but only Mies obtained a patent. And it was a wise move. Income from the MR and a later simpler chair supported the designer through many years when architectural commissions were few and far between.

The exhibition was virtually a study in advanced theories of construction and design. Its success seems even more startling when we consider its sponsors: a small, provincial city and an organization of artists and industrialists, both within a defeated and poverty-stricken country. Even the Nazis could not dim the exhibition's luster. Alarmed by its progressiveness, they declared the development "degenerate architecture." And upon coming to power in 1933, they tried to degrade the whole project with picture postcards labeling it "Arab Village, Stuttgart."

Mies had produced for Stuttgart not only his interesting apartment house but also a dazzling display of German glassware. Its impact on most viewers was probably similar to the effect it had much later on architect Howard Dearstyne: "It was in 1928 or 1929 that I came upon a photograph of this project, the first work of Mies van der Rohe that I had ever seen. . . . Mies had seen fit to display the industry's project in the form of floor-to-ceiling-height walls of clear, etched and green glass so arranged that they formed a room giving out on a court. I well remember how impressed I was by the somber beauty of this space composition. And I wondered who Mies van der Rohe was."

Typically, though, Mies recognized others' achievements

much more clearly than his own. In 1953, at a seventieth birthday party for Walter Gropius, he rose to pay what, for him, was
a wordy tribute: "I am glad I had once the possibility in
Stuttgart to give Gropius a hand so that he could demonstrate
his ideas on industrialization and prefabrication. He built two
houses there which were the most interesting ones in the
exhibit."

Besides advancing the cause of modern architecture and
participants like Gropius, the exhibition landed practicing architect van der Rohe a juicy official commission.

German authorities, impressed with Mies's buildings and or-
ganizational skills at Stuttgart, approached him about designing
the German pavilion for an international exposition at Barcelona, Spain. In a 1965 interview, a bemused Mies reminisced
about this: "You know, there were already seventeen enormous
general buildings—really palaces—planned for the exhibition
when representatives of the German government heard that
France and England were each putting up separate national
pavilions. So they decided to have one, too. I asked, 'For what
purpose?' They said, 'We don't know—just build a pavilion, but
not too much glass!' "

From such a vague, brief directive came a masterpiece, what
many have called one of the most beautiful and influential
designs of the twentieth century. Indeed, the very lack of program probably contributed to its greatness. Mies confirmed this
later when he said the project was his most difficult but also his
most creative, because he was his own client, could do what he
liked, and had no advance inkling of what a pavilion should be.

The first thing he did was to give free rein to his imagination
and his ideals of classical perfection. There would be no exhibit
within his pavilion, he decided. The building itself would be the
exhibit. So unique was Mies's creation that it almost defies
description, and we have only photographs to help, for the
small one-story jewel was hardly there before it was gone—it
was taken down immediately at the end of the exposition.

The pavilion was more "architectural space" than structure.
It consisted of walls and columns set on a low podium, between
which, said one observer poetically, "the building happened

like a slow dance." The hovering roof was supported by eight cross-shaped steel columns sheathed in chrome, freeing the glass and marble walls from any bearing duties. Use of travertine, onyx, gray glass, and green Tinian marble lent an intrinsic beauty. The pavilion's only adornments were two reflecting pools lined with black glass; a sculpture, "Dancer" by Georg Kolbe; and furniture designed by the architect. Among the furniture was Mies's chrome, steel, and leather Barcelona chair, considered by many to be his most beautiful design. It was also his most ample—big enough to accommodate two. Van der Rohe, quite ample himself, confessed he'd designed it with his own comfort in mind.

The dean of all central European architects, Peter Behrens, journeyed to Barcelona expressly to see the pavilion. Mies later liked to repeat proudly his old teacher's first reaction to the building: "My heart leaped up." Not too many were to get the chance Behrens had to view the structure. The dismantled pieces of the pavilion were supposedly shipped back to Germany, but Mies was never able to trace them. Fortunately, widely published photos established Mies's mastery so conclusively that even if he had died that summer of his forty-third year, his position would have been secure.

The one other building that, along with the Barcelona pavilion, is considered to be the apex of van der Rohe's European career is the Tugendhat house erected in 1930 in Brno, Czechoslovakia.

"It is very curious how buildings come to pass," Mies remarked on one occasion. This is certainly true of the way the cautious, rather conservative Tugendhats ended up with one of the most uncompromising statements of modern architecture around.

The couple seemed to come by the distinguished residence almost in spite of themselves. But let the architect tell the story, as he often did, with dry wit and irony: "Mr. Tugendhat came to me. He was a very careful man. He did not believe in one doctor only—he had three. He picked me out for a curious reason: he saw a house I built when I was very young. It was very well built, and he expected something similar.

"I went there and saw the situation. I designed the house. I remember it was Christmas Eve when he saw the design. He nearly died. But his wife was interested in art. She had some Van Gogh pictures; she said, 'Let us think it over.' . . . He said he did not like the open space; it would be too disturbing. People would be there when he was in the library with his great thoughts. He was a businessman, I think. On New Year's Eve he came to me and told me I should go ahead."

According to Mrs. Tugendhat, though, she and her husband still had no inkling of what they were getting until the actual building was sitting there. "We couldn't read architectural drawings very well," she confessed.

There was another fracas over the interior decoration. Mies had designed it all, even down to door handles and curtain tracks. Then the client announced, "I give in on everything, but not about the furniture." Van der Rohe replied calmly, "This is too bad," and proceeded to send his superintendent with the truck of furniture to the newly built house anyway.

"He [Tugendhat] will be furious at first," Mies warned his workman, "but you must expect that."

As predicted, the client shouted "Take it out" when he saw the first piece going in. But by afternoon he liked it all. The exasperated architect concluded, "I think we should treat our clients as children."

Several years later one of Mies's students who was visiting Brno was received graciously in the great open living room by the lady of the house. "At first, the place disturbed us," she admitted. "It took some time adjusting to, but now we are beginning to enjoy this way of living."

Mies always maintained that anyone who could design a good house could design anything. For the Tugendhats he designed one of the best. It was the first glass house. Its windows and glass sliding panels reached from floor to ceiling so that the outside greenery formed the boundaries. According to architectural critics, this house was to Mies's development what the Robie house was to Wright's and the Villa Savoye to Le Corbusier's.

Mies's personality and his ideas about building were evident throughout. The open plan of the main living floor was an impressive statement of his conception of space. The interior, among the most beautiful ever designed, showed how skillfully he could contrast rich materials with restrained materials. The perfection of each visible element was evidence of his scrupulous attention to detail—he designed everything from furniture to hardware, even the heating pipes. The terrace and the flight of steps connecting the residence to the garden below illustrated his classical bent. His juxtaposition of geometry with nature—he framed the house between level courts carved out of the slope—showed how effectively he could treat a site architecturally. And the muted colors apparent throughout demonstrated Mies's extreme sensitivity to color.

The Tugendhat home was entered from the top floor. Situated on a sloping hill, the building provided a superb view of the town. The rooms on the upper level—five bedrooms, a garage, and chauffeur's quarters—were closed (for privacy) and conventional. But the bottom living level was open, elegant, and revolutionary. The whole plan was mixed: half open and half closed, partly bearing wall and partly skeleton construction.

A circular glass staircase led from the upper entrance hall down to the main floor below. A hundred feet of glass opened living and dining areas to view. At the push of a button, panels slid down into basement pockets like automobile windows to transform the living room into a semi-enclosed terrace.

Curtains made of black silk, natural silk, and white velvet could be drawn to regulate the light. Mies, always a man of understatement, preferred the natural colors of the landscape to any bright hues. He used mainly whites and off whites, blacks and off blacks. Recalling his first trip to Italy, he said, "The sun and the blue skies were so bright, I thought I'd go crazy. I couldn't wait to go back to the North, where everything was gray and subtle."

The gray and slightly grim, contrastless tone in the pictures of his 1920s German structures pleased Mies so much that he always tried to get the same effect when commissioning photography of his American work.

Like the Barcelona pavilion, the hillside house had H-shaped chromium columns supporting the roof. Areas for sitting, dining, studying, card-playing, and conversing were delineated by one straight wall of tawny gold and white onyx, and a curved one of striped black and brown ebony. Linoleum and a natural wool rug, both white, covered different areas of the floor.

Inside the home, Mies carefully placed more furniture of his own design. Besides his Barcelona chairs and stools, there was a glass-topped table braced on crossed, chromium-plated steel bars. And there were special Tugendhat chairs, upholstered versions of his patented cantilevered chairs. These were done in white vellum, natural pigskin, and pale green cowhide.

A bust on a square pedestal formed the focal point of an island of open space in the living area. The sculpture was by Wilhelm Lehmbruck, a personal friend whose work van der Rohe admired. He had wanted the Lehmbruck piece "Kneeling Woman" for the court of his Barcelona pavilion but had been unable to borrow it. He eventually took a taxi to the studio of another sculptor, Georg Kolbe, and quickly chose a substitute work. Because of Mies's impeccable taste, the figure fit beautifully in its setting. As a result, there were rumors that Kolbe and van der Rohe had collaborated. Those who advocate such collaboration between architects and other creative agents like painters and sculptors even cite the Barcelona pavilion as a good example. "Actually," said Mies, "in the initial designs of my buildings I do not believe there can be cooperation between the artist and the architect. The reason is simple: my structural objectives always have an objective character, never subjective. I get along well with artists, but their work has nothing to do with my work."

Gropius, upon seeing the Tugendhat house, called it a "Sunday house," and it earned plaudits around the world. But the architect who built it treated the accomplishment rather nonchalantly: "I think it is considered outstanding only because it was the first modern house to use rich materials, to have great elegance. At that time modern buildings were still austerely functional. I personally don't consider the Tugendhat house more important than the other works that I designed considerably earlier."

After World War II, during which the house was damaged, local Czech authorities converted it into a gymnasium with parallel bars along the walls, and painted its white linoleum red. Upon seeing a snapshot of the changed structure, Mies grinned and said, "You know, it doesn't look bad at all!"

For the Berlin Building Exposition of 1931, he designed a full-sized house and a bachelor's apartment. In 1933 his was the only modern plan among six prizewinners in a competition for the new Reichsbank in Berlin. This winning design, like one he submitted four years later for an administration building for the silk industry in Krefeld, was symmetrical on a monumental scale.

Mies's last years in Germany—1931 to 1938—were taken up mainly by a series of designs for houses with courtyards. Glass-walled and shaped in the form of L's, T's or I's, the courtyards were a contemporary version of the inner patio of Roman times. Many eloquent and detailed sketches reveal this to be one of the themes most exhaustively studied by Mies. These drawings inspired a whole new generation of architects.

However, in Germany the 1930s were lean years for modernists. Clients were favoring architects who conformed to the Hitler-imposed building patterns. So only the Lencke house—a small L on a narrow Berlin lot—actually went up under van der Rohe's direction. But his achievements were recognized in other ways. In 1930 he was appointed director of the Bauhaus in Dessau, and in 1931 he was made a member of the Prussian Academy of Arts and Sciences. His designs and models began to draw throngs of fans to museums around the world. And though he was reluctant to give public speeches, he was invited to do so by more and more organizations.

Of all this recognition, Mies probably valued the Bauhaus appointment most. The Bauhaus (House of Building) had been changed by his friend Gropius from a typical arts and crafts school into the first serious workshop for the development of industrial art. Under the slogan "Art and Technology—The New Unity," the school had amazingly upgraded European product design in just one decade. Not only had Gropius assembled a staff of the finest designers, artists, and architects to teach at the workshop; he had designed for it at Dessau an extraordinary complex of buildings, including one sheathed entirely in glass. Unfortunately the school became a political football, and director Gropius felt forced to resign in 1928. He was succeeded by architect Hannes Meyer. But Meyer's two-year term was filled with such unrest that Dessau authorities decided the only way to get the Bauhaus back in working order was to appoint a director recommended by Gropius. The recommendation was Mies van der Rohe.

Followers of Meyer were indignant. They labeled Mies "a bourgeois formalist." They demanded that he show them an exhibit of his work so they could judge his qualifications. Instead, van der Rohe turned the tables. He closed the school for three months and personally judged each student's qualifications. Each was questioned by the architect in his office. One of those interviewed was the American Dearstyne, who was later to teach at the Illinois Institute of Technology. "When my turn came, I was at a loss to find something to say to van der Rohe," he recalled. "Since, however, I had chafed under the sterile functionalism of Hannes Meyer, I asked Mies if it were not still possible to strive for beauty in architecture. I didn't know the man to whom I was talking when I asked that question. 'Of course,' he said, 'it is still possible.' "

When the new Bauhaus director had finished his interviews, he thought all refractory elements had been weeded out. Then a delegation marched into his office, announcing that there would be a student strike immediately unless he met certain demands. Staring coldly at the emissaries, Mies said, "You are here to work and learn. Anyone not present at his classes in the morning will be expelled."

Under van der Rohe's direction, the Bauhaus soon settled down to being the workshop that Gropius, its founder, had intended it to be. Mies instituted the approach he was later to use at the Illinois Institute of Technology. Abandoning the tradition of individual prizes in competitions, Mies sternly told his students, "First you have to learn something; then you can go out and do it." Using the atrium and row houses as a medium of instruction, he stressed structure, space, proportion, and use of materials.

For two years everything ran comparatively smoothly. Then a Nazi governor and a Nazi legislature took control in Anhalt, the province where Dessau was located. These authorities had an ultraconservative architect pass judgment on the Bauhaus. Mies was attacked for teaching "degenerate" and "un-German" ideas. Regretfully, the director abandoned the splendid Dessau workshop buildings and set up the Bauhaus in an empty factory in Berlin.

But then Hitler came to power, and by the fall of 1933 the school was being maligned even more viciously in Berlin than it had been in Dessau. Finally Mies arrived one morning to find the doors of the factory padlocked. While anxious friends and students gathered in a nearby restaurant, the director went to discuss the matter with Nazi "Cultural Expert" Alfred Rosenberg, who finally agreed to reopen the Bauhaus. Those in the restaurant greeted this news with elation, and drinks were passed all around.

Then Mies announced, "Now that they've agreed to let us stay open, let's close up." The school could not continue to exist in such an atmosphere, he maintained. So close it he did. The Bauhaus, in its original form, ended forever that day.

Mies remained in Germany for four more years, sketching a variety of designs and working privately with a few Bauhaus students. At forty-seven he did not welcome the idea of starting over in any other country, particularly since he spoke only German. But there were no royalties coming in on his books, and the Nazis were becoming increasingly hostile to everything he represented. So when, in 1937, an offer came to design a house in the more hospitable climate of America, Mies accepted. It was an invitation he couldn't afford to refuse.

New Land, New Career

When Mies began contemplating a move to the United States, it was not as though the man and the country were complete strangers.

"The most important idea in modern architecture is the skeletal idea developed in Chicago," the architect stated often. And he readily admitted that photographs of steel skyscrapers then under construction in Chicago and Manhattan had inspired his own steel and glass tower designs of the 1920s. He was also quick to praise United States engineers for articulating the language of modern building even before architects. On visiting New York, he never failed to stop and admire the George Washington Bridge, which he called "the most modern building in the city"—praiseworthy for its beautiful proportions and its honesty in materials.

As for Americans, progressives had already become impressed with Mies's tough and elegant work. Critic-historian Henry-Russell Hitchcock and architect Philip Johnson, an admirer and friend, had included van der Rohe's buildings in an exhibit of international architecture that they had arranged for the Museum of Modern Art in 1932. And, of course, word of his accomplishments had been coming to this country with regularity.

It is nevertheless startling to realize that this fame that preceded Mies was based on a far smaller body of work than that of

Gropius, Le Corbusier, and Wright. By 1937, when Mies arrived here, he had to his credit a sum total of twenty-seven building projects, only eleven of which had been executed. And one of the most important of these—the Barcelona pavilion—had been so small and ephemeral that it was gone almost before anyone realized its significance. And there were no books by van der Rohe to propagandize his achievements. Only a few short articles had appeared under his byline. And though some singular honors had come his way, such as his brief directorship of the Bauhaus, this architect was never one to blow his own horn.

It was architect Philip Johnson who suggested to the Stanley Resors of the J. Walter Thompson Advertising Agency that they commission van der Rohe to design a country house for them in Wyoming. This was actually to be Mies's second project in this country. In 1930 he had designed a New York apartment for Johnson. The German architect arrived here in the summer of 1937 to survey the Resors' spectacular site in Jackson Hole, Wyoming. The terrain called for a design radically different from the court types he'd been experimenting with in his native country.

For the Resors, Mies designed a low, rectangular box that spanned a stream, resting at either end on stone piers. But it was hardly the usual rectangular box house. Though bedrooms and service areas were closed, the extended living-dining area had full-height window walls that provided a view of the mountain scenery in both directions. So despite the rigid restraints of the shape, the living area had all the free-flowing openness and spaciousness of his earlier domestic architecture. This plan—consolidation into a single rectangle containing a regular system of supports—was actually a preview of Mies's later work in America.

As usual, the architect paid close attention to details and used rich materials. The structure's steel and wood frame was covered with cypress plank. Bronze sheathed the interior columns. And the fireplace was of random ashlar masonry. But for the most part, architectural elements in this house were underplayed to give top booking to the view. The studies done for this home were probably Mies's clearest demonstration of how important he felt landscape to be in glass architecture.

The Resor home, unfortunately, was never built. But this trip to the United States was to produce one of those accidental sets of circumstances that would lead van der Rohe to the full flowering of his career. He deserved a bit of luck. So far, forces not of his own making had adversely influenced his work: first World War I, then the rise of the Nazis.

On a trip through Chicago, Mies happened to meet John Holabird, one of the city's leading architects. Holabird was looking for a man to head the School of Architecture at Chicago's Armour Institute. (Later Armour merged with Lewis Institute to form the Illinois Institute of Technology.)

Impressed with the German builder, Holabird phoned Armour president Henry Heald: "I don't really know Mies van der Rohe," he admitted, "but the Barcelona pavilion and one or two other things he has done are outstanding. And, after all, even if we don't know too much about this fellow, he's so much better than any of the other people you could get to head a school of architecture, why not take a chance?"

Heald agreed. Mies was offered the job. Asked his terms, he replied, "A completely free hand and ten thousand dollars a year." The Institute couldn't quite afford the requested salary, but it guaranteed him free rein in developing a completely new teaching program. So van der Rohe accepted and moved to the United States permanently. And for twenty years—1938 to 1958—he was Director of Architecture at the Institute.

"I still remember the first day he came to my office on the old campus at Illinois Tech," recalled Heald, who later became president of the Ford Foundation. "He couldn't speak English, and my German was far from adequate, so we sat and looked at each other until one of our professors who had a mastery of German came in to interpret for us. That was our introduction to each other."

Heald soon found that his was the only American school of architecture to do its teaching in German. "Mies, a perfectionist, was reluctant to use English in the classroom," explained the Institute president. "It was not until after Pearl

Harbor that he did. I remember having lunch with him shortly after the beginning of the war. Somehow the question of language came up, and I said, 'Why don't you start using English in your teaching?' He said, 'Very well, we start now.' And he did. Never after that did he do his teaching in German, and of course he soon became quite articulate in English."

But language was still a barrier on what was supposed to be a festive occasion held soon after van der Rohe's arrival in this country. It was a dinner at Chicago's Palmer House, where the new director was to be presented to the Armour faculty and trustees. Those present remember it as a nightmare. Mies, who abhorred such duties, had finally agreed to make his first speech in America, but only in his native tongue. The president of the American Institute of Architects—a man who prided himself on his German—was to translate for the audience. It soon became apparent, however, that the translator's German and Mies's German were not from the same book. The AIA head stuttered and stumbled and finally became completely bogged down.

This first unhappy experience with an American audience discouraged Mies from further public speaking. Heald said, "As president of Illinois Tech, I used to think it would be nice to parade this ornament on our faculty, and I would schedule him as main speaker for this or that event. But usually, as the date approached, it became evident that one of his associates was going to take his place. When I questioned Mies, his answer was, 'Well, we do a good job and people will know about it. We don't need to tell them.'"

In other respects, though, van der Rohe and IIT seemed to hit it off at once. In his twenty years there, not only did he develop one of the nation's top architectural schools, but he was entrusted with the planning and designing of the entire campus. Not every architecture dean is called upon for advice on building in his own university, and few modern architects have had the chance to design on such a large scale.

Mies and his adopted country also got along well from the beginning. It has often been said that only Europe could have produced him, but only America could have provided him with

the chance to fully realize his ideas. Although he was over fifty
when he settled here, the architect grasped almost intuitively
the nature of modern building technology favored in the United States. So completely did his buildings demonstrate new
construction techniques—exposed steel framing, modular rep-
etition, and the refined detailing of machine-produced
materials—that it's hard to believe a newcomer to our shores
designed them. Probably in no other land except the steel-
building United States could Mies's talents have been employed
so immediately and directly "with scarcely a dropped stitch in
the changeover," as one critic has noted.

Perhaps the successful transplanting can be attributed to the
fact that in many ways van der Rohe was more American than
Americans: in his Puritan-like emphasis on spiritual values and
traditional morals, for example, and in the no-nonsense precision and purity of his plans. Whatever the reasons, many more
of his designs turned into actual buildings here than in Europe.
And his American work, unlike his earlier projects, attracted
followers from all over the world.

One of Mies's wisest decisions was to settle in Chicago rather
than another city. As historian James Marston Fitch has said,
"Who better than this poet of glass and steel could have carried
on the skyscraper tradition of this city?" With its assortment of
Sullivan and Wright buildings, Chicago was certainly more
receptive to architectural innovations than most cities. And van
der Rohe, for his part, must have found it exciting to be working in an area whose structures had first inspired him as a
young apprentice. "In 1912, when I was working in The
Hague," he told one interviewer, "I first saw a drawing by Louis
Sullivan of one of his buildings. It interested me. And before I
came to Chicago I also knew about Frank Lloyd Wright and
particularly about his Robie house. . . . Their work was very
important."

Yet Mies always maintained that he would have created the
same things had he stayed in Germany. He denied that living in
Chicago had produced any effects. Once, when asked if prox-
imity to the Chicago School (a group of architects practicing a
particular kind of building in the Chicago area) had changed

his thinking and construction pattern, he replied, "No. I really don't know the Chicago School. You see, I never walk. I always take taxis back and forth to work. I rarely see the city." Nevertheless, Mies's grandson and later close collaborator, Dirk Lohan, said, "I personally believe that the special climate and pace of Chicago helped him to create what he did."

The architect's life in this country was a solitary, unpretentious one. He moved into a spacious apartment in an old building on Chicago's North Side, about a block from Lake Michigan. The tenant, a gourmet, made sure his kitchen was well equipped for the use of his cook. But the rest of the rooms remained unfurnished except for several Mies chairs; a couple of non-Mies upholstered black sofas, usually covered with blueprints and ruled drawings; an occasional marble shelf, on one of which stood a Hallicrafters radio, its wire straggling down to the baseboard; and some thick mats on the floor. On the stark white walls hung bright, carefully lit paintings by his favorite artist, Klee, and a few photographs of his buildings.

Mies lived a monastic kind of life, often reading through the night about science and philosophy "to find out what is essential in our time." Reading, staring at his extensive art collection, partaking of good meals, and puffing away at his giant cigars were the main pleasures of this gentleman architect. He kept rather peculiar schedules, rising late in the day, seldom speaking before lunch, and never retiring before the wee hours of the morning. Friends and acquaintances knew better than to phone the architect before eleven A.M. And although his daytime communication was often limited to grunts and a smile or two between cigar puffs, at night after dinner he could come alive if the atmosphere was right. Then, with drink in hand, he could become quite cheerful, sometimes even talkative. He loved reminiscing about his early days as a plasterer's helper, or about his later years as Bauhaus head, or about his automobile tour of the United States in the 1940s with architect friend Konrad Wachsman.

"Not only presence but personage" is how author Richard Stern described Mies. "A wonderful talker, ebullient, a fountain of ease, his great arched head tilting in the humor of things with memories, comment, hospitality." Most people who did get close to van der Rohe found this same simplicity and friendliness. But not too many got this close. There was about him a mystique, an aura; he seemed to personify the conscience of the architectural profession. Partly this was due to his daytime reticence and shyness. Partly it stemmed from the zealous way in which associates tended to shield him from the outside world. But mostly it was a result of the regard and respect he aroused in his own architectural students, who tended to spread their awe and hero worship to others.

"True education is concerned not only with practical goals but also with values," said Mies in his IIT inaugural address. "In its simplest form, architecture is rooted in entirely functional considerations, but it can reach up through all degrees of value to the highest sphere of spiritual existence, into the realm of pure art."

In line with this belief, the architect established a program at IIT that was as demanding as that of any religious order. Only the most serious and singleminded were accepted and allowed to remain. Students had to meet the strict standards of draftsmanship and structural knowledge that Mies had been trained to require of himself.

Some felt this resulted in "the most rigid and formal school in America." To this criticism Mies replied, "I see no rigidness in the curriculum at all. We try to teach students awareness about the problems involved. We don't teach them solutions; we teach them a way to solve problems."

This way had to be universal, objective, and anonymous, van der Rohe felt. "You know, when I came here to the school and I had to change the curriculum, I was just thinking to find a method which teaches the student how to make a good building. Nothing else.

"First, we taught them how to draw. The first year is spent on that. And they learn how to draw. Then we taught them construction in stone, in brick, in wood, and made them learn something about engineering. We talked about concrete and steel. Then we taught them something about functions of buildings, and in the junior year we tried to teach them a sense of proportion and sense of space. And only in the last year we came to a group of buildings."

The way Mies set up his course seems very logical. It was based on a "you have to learn to walk before you can run" theory. But the reaction in his day was amazement. Associate Professor of Architecture Daniel Brenner said visitors to IIT were impressed and puzzled by the clear philosophy guiding the school and by the simple, direct, and consequential manner in which one study built upon another. The main surprise was that the rigorous training had little to do with education for design. "The word design is not used at IIT," Brenner explained. "There is too much in it of the arbitrary, the self-conscious and the superficial."

When Mies outlined his curriculum for historian Nikolaus Pevsner, editor of the British *Architectural Review,* who was conducting a survey on architectural teaching methods used throughout the world, Pevsner was shocked. Thinking the IIT director had misunderstood, he sent another questionnaire. Mies merely described his program in greater detail.

At a time when schools were still clinging to traditional methods of instruction, Pevsner's shock was understandable. Only van der Rohe at IIT and Wright at Taliesin expected a student to know something about structure and material before he took pen in hand to design, say, a skyscraper. Both believed you could teach technique, general principles, a sense of order and proportion, and how to use reason—but after that, it was up to the individual student himself.

Mies's classes were conducted in seminar fashion, ten to twelve in a group. "He was never wildly physically active, and he did not do much talking," recalled one pupil. This was an understatement, to say the least. Mies stayed so quietly in the background that a group of students, tongue in cheek, requested that a Christmas party be held at the Institute so they could meet the director.

"Some students you simply cannot teach," admitted Mies. "What's important is not to act as if everyone is a genius. As I have often said, architecture starts when you carefully put two bricks together. There it begins." He believed that of the twenty aspirants admitted every year to IIT, if two were really good they could change Chicago. And if there were ten of this caliber over a number of years, the whole cultural climate could be changed. A generation of young men trained by Mies in the classical disciplines now head the staffs of many American architectural offices. And through them the Miesian style has found multiple expressions across the land.

While he was conducting his classes, Mies was also getting a chance to design the new physical facilities for the Institute. This was due to an act of God, you might say. The architect originally commissioned, a board of trustees member, had died, and staunch supporter Henry Heald backed Mies for the job. He probably never would have gotten the commission otherwise. "In fact," said the Institute president, "after we began to execute Mies's designs, I recall meeting with a committee of the faculty who said, in effect, 'Are you sure you shouldn't have your head examined for being a party to this construction?' This was after the first building was built. The sun shone in on one side, and it didn't have any closets, and there were other points which bothered the professors. Nevertheless, Mies proceeded with the total design of the campus."

And despite all the criticisms, Heald always declared that the architect's campus design "was one of the most, perhaps *the* most significant thing that ever happened to Illinois Institute of Technology," especially considering the limitations under which Mies labored.

There were so many limitations that several associates and admirers felt Mies deserved a better client. The first difficulty was the site—"miserable for its purposes, restricted by railroads and the gridiron pattern of streets," observed one friend. The area was one of the worst slums in the country. At first glimpse of it, admitted van der Rohe, he was tempted to turn around and go home to Germany. Instead he turned to Heald and said, "It can't be any worse. So it's a great challenge. I'd like to work on such a group of buildings."

A second difficulty was money. The Institute had little of it then. In management of his personal income, said friends, Mies was too generous with office staff and too liberal in spending for designs likely never to see the light of day.

But for IIT the architect showed great ability to save money when pressure was on. His meticulous attention to detail left nothing to chance. Sometimes he foresaw clearly that a certain thrifty shortcut or substitution would be disastrous, and he would point this out. Usually he was proved correct, as when a proposed majestic granite slab at the entrance of one building was replaced with a cheaper ordinary concrete one, totally spoiling the effect.

Before long, van der Rohe had also proved he was not the hard-to-work-with and inflexible architect he was sometimes accused of being. "In the process of building," Dr. Heald once remarked, "when we would discuss a particular problem, Mies's answer would be, 'Well, we'll think about it.' That's the difference between Mies and a good many other architects I know. He *would* think about it and come back with a solution."

In his original IIT plan (a preliminary version in 1939, and a master one in 1941), van der Rohe suggested removing the long center street from the rectangular site—eight blocks on Chicago's South Side—and closing the interior streets. Then some twenty assorted buildings—libraries and labs, machine shops, classroom structures, and the like—would form a unified group around an open plaza. To increase the sense of openness and spaciousness without destroying the frame of the plaza, many of the peripheral buildings would be raised on exposed steel columns. And two fan-shaped auditoriums were to serve as diverting points in the rectangular plan.

But Mies was told, "You can't simply eliminate a main thoroughfare and close off all those avenues." (Although several were closed afterwards, when it was too late, because construction was already underway.) The architect merely shrugged his shoulders and showed the same flexibility he'd shown officials at the exhibit at Stuttgart many years before. He produced another plan, incorporating clusters of smaller buildings within the previous symmetrical scheme.

Always a master at arranging space, Mies now did it on a

grand urban scale for the first time. He conceived of twenty buildings grouped in a series of quadrangles, subtly interlocked so that visitors were led easily from one court to the next. Just as he'd overlapped wall planes in the Barcelona pavilion and Tugendhat house, he overlapped planes and columns of his campus buildings so that beyond each one, another became visible in the distance. The effect was that of each structure "sliding out from the building in front of it," suggesting an unseen continuity of space beyond.

"Modern buildings of our time are so huge," van der Rohe said much later in his career, "that one must group them. Often the space between these buildings is as important as the buildings themselves. And how these buildings are related to each other. You can see an example of this here in Chicago. In the group of apartments between 860 and 900 Lake Shore Drive, we purposely opened up the surrounding and intervening space; now the space is being filled up with additional buildings. How ridiculous!"

Mies's first campus building was completed in 1943; eleven more were to go up during the next thirteen years before he retired. Grasping immediately the new steel construction language of American building, he employed a steel frame with panels of brick or glass. Each structure repeated the standard unit. Behind the identical rectangular facades, though, there were a variety of spaces—open workshops, research labs, boiler rooms, classrooms. And he avoided monotony by his emphatic treatment of corners. One authority has said, "The corner detail is the best known and certainly one of the most influential of Mies's American contributions."

But one Chicago architect, viewing the first IIT buildings, commented that they all looked to him like warehouses thrown up by some contractor. To the uninitiated, most of Mies's buildings, regardless of function, do look amazingly alike. He deliberately aimed at such universality and impersonality. Architecture has to express its time, he said. In a day when functions were changing so rapidly, the old slogan "form follows function" was obsolete. The important thing was to create "universal structures" adjustable to tomorrow's requirements, as valid for the future as for the present.

"Novelty doesn't interest me," announced van der Rohe on more than one occasion. "If it were necessary to make curves, I would make curves. But as long as we have this same economic and scientific structure, steel will be the essence of our cities. Our buildings need not look alike. After all, there are about ten thousand species of seashells. They don't look alike, but they have the same principle."

Of the dozen campus structures that Mies actually built, his personal favorite was Crown Hall, a single glass-walled room, a hundred and twenty feet by two hundred and twenty feet, spanned by four huge tresses. In line with his conception of universal buildings, he used movable partitions that could be shifted. But there is one problem with these partitions. Since they are not carried all the way to the ceiling plane, there are acoustics and lighting difficulties. For example, in Crown Hall—now the School of Architecture and Design—cut-off panels separate the drafting room, and every time a student moves his drafting stool, annoying squeaks are audible in other parts of the building.

Meanwhile, Mies's creations went up one by one on the IIT campus—the Metals Research Building, the Engineering Research Building, Alumni Memorial Hall, Perlstein Hall, and Wishnick Hall. What would probably have been his most brilliant of the series, however, was never built. This was his monumental library-administration hall, which was to have an enormous interior court, a two-story library, and a cantilevered mezzanine within a two-story public space—all behind what would have been the largest exterior glass walls ever produced in this country.

By the time the architect had reached the Institute's arbitrary retirement age in 1958, only twelve of his proposed twenty campus buildings had been erected. His supporter Heald had left for New York, and the Ford Foundation and a new administration decided to give other architects a chance. They approached a firm headed by an old friend of Mies. This architect promptly turned around and invited Mies to help design the new IIT buildings, but as an associate under his firm's banner. Mies declined: "I don't want to come in through the back door. And anyway, the whole campus is already designed. Why not just carry it out?"

Nevertheless, Institute students ran a full-page protest in their campus paper. The architect thanked them but professed himself too busy to fight about the remaining IIT structures. And he was.

Already he had created many "firsts" and prototypes: his glass and steel office building designs; his concrete house, which was a harbinger of the California ranch house; his court homes, which reintroduced the Roman atrium into modern architecture in the form of a patio; his use of screens and cabinets as wall dividers; and his pioneering designs for the tubular furniture that is so popular today.

But in his last two decades of life, Mies van der Rohe, with an amazing spurt of energy, was to come up with expressions of even greater inventiveness.

"A glacial continuity . . ."

"We came upon Mies sitting silently in the partitionless space of one of his Lake Shore Drive apartments," recalled one visitor. "His head wreathed in cigar smoke, he was studying a tentative division of the space indicated by a roll of paper hung from the ceiling. We stopped by two hours later, and he evidently had not moved except to sigh thoughtfully and light another cigar."

This was how Mies worked. First there was a period of unin-

terrupted contemplation, usually within the privacy of his own
rooms. Then, intermittently, came numerous small sketches
(for his Bacardi building in Cuba, he made more than one
hundred detailed studies of the profile of the eight concrete
columns supporting the roof). Next these drawings were taken
to the small white-walled architectural office he opened soon
after he was commissioned by IIT. Like his apartment, it was
sparsely furnished: one of his 1930 Brno chairs, a few tables,
and some pictures of his buildings. There he would examine
scale models and full-sized mock-ups of structure parts produced in a well-equipped workshop. A purist, he tried with
every fiber of his being to reduce the work to its very essence,
eliminating every irrelevant feature. *"Beinahe nichts*—almost nothing," he kept reminding his assistants as he directed this
change or that. This simplification process could consume
weeks or months, and all the while few words were spoken.
Often the only sounds were the scrape of pen on paper and
Mies's regular puffing at his ever-present cigar. "It had all the
atmosphere," said one observer, "of an operating room where a
great surgeon is preparing to perform a revolutionary operation for the first time."

In order to concentrate singlemindedly on a design, the
architect sublimated all the superficial concerns that distract
and sap the energies of most people. Friends and associates
were often astounded at how unperturbed Mies would remain
while storms of controversy and criticism swirled around him.

But then there came some fireworks on the order of those
that usually surrounded Wright and Le Corbusier. And van der
Rohe, in spite of himself, was drawn into lawsuits, debates,
verbal recriminations, denunciations in the press, and all sorts
of unpleasant developments that he usually sought to avoid at
all costs.

In 1946 Dr. Edith Farnsworth, a Chicago physician and a
close friend of the architect for several years, bought some
wooded land on the Fox River in Plano, Illinois. Mies set about
designing a house for her. It took him six years, but the result
was one of the most beautiful and most important houses of the
twentieth century. Lifted on stilts to avoid the periodic flooding

of the river, the house seemed to "float" above its territory. It has been called "a little building of ravishing grace and elegance."

Someone described the Farnsworth place as a "quantity of air caught between the floor and the roof." It is simply a single rectangular room bound on all four sides by glass. Only a travertine floor and the rippling reflections of the outside greenery on the glass walls provide relief from its rigid form, white frames, white plaster ceiling, white silk curtains, and white movable partitions. It, more than any of his other creations, embodies his favorite "less is more" maxim (which Mies scrupulously denied originating and always credited to Peter Behrens).

But Dr. Farnsworth, after living briefly in her new home, wrote angrily in *House Beautiful,* "We now know that 'less is *not* more.' It is simply less!" The house cost too much to build (about seventy-three thousand dollars) and to maintain and was simply not livable, she declared. She further charged that Mies's design had made no concession to one of the most difficult climates on earth, an area with subpolar winters and Congo-like hot and humid summers.

It was the same old bugaboos the architect had faced before—the problems of light and temperature. Since all the walls were of unshaded glass, the glare was often severe. This was especially true in winter when the ground was covered with snow. Drawing the curtains brought relief, conceded the lady, but also cut off the view, which was the reason for the glass in the first place.

Also, there was only one pair of doors, there was no air-conditioning, and there were no openable windows. When direct sunlight penetrated the unshaded glass, inside temperatures rose to an ovenlike degree even in winter, reported Mrs. Farnsworth, and moving out into the home's beautiful porch and "floating" terrace was no solution because of the absence of insect screens.

Before the fracas was over, others had joined in the attack, including architects like Wright. Mies, Corbu and Gropius, aided and abetted by the Museum of Modern Art, were trying to foist the barren, grim, cold "international style" of architecture on Americans, accusers said. There was even a hint that communists were behind the whole thing.

Mies's friendship with Dr. Farnsworth was irrevocably ended. The lawsuits were decided in his favor. She herself made some careful modifications which increased the home's livability, such as screening the outside porch. But, said one visitor after the alterations, "Mies's beautiful creation has been not merely maimed, but destroyed. Where once pure space flowed between and around those hovering planes, there is now a solid black tube, heavy and inert."

The architect's loyal defenders argued that the Farnsworth home was never meant to be a typical, practical "house for everyday family living." It was intended to be a perfect, costly showcase for a woman living alone. Even some of Wright's and Le Corbusier's clients found their dwellings too expensive and inefficient, Mies's fans pointed out. Yet they'd never swap for a more economical, functional piece of mediocrity.

With great insight, architectural scholar James Marston Fitch pinpointed the crux of the difficulty: "Mies has created an architectural order, imperturbable and implacable (the adjectives are those of his admirers), for an ideal landscape. Nothing ever happens here. It is airless, timeless, filled with light—but not sunlight. . . . No gales howl here, no dust blows, no insects fly. . . . There is no weather in his compassless world. In sum, Mies designs for the golden climate of Plato's Republic—but he builds in Mayor Daley's Chicago."

Of course, the architect must have become increasingly aware of this dilemma. But, shocked and annoyed by his critics, he also became increasingly stubborn. For many years he refused to take into account the mundane problems of practical living.

"You cannot substitute climate control for architecture," he'd declare testily. And when asked about air-conditioning or garbage collection, he'd say, "That is not my métier." In one of his rare speeches, an address in 1950 at IIT, he took this sly jab at the Institute of Design: "Some people are convinced that architecture will be outmoded and replaced by technology. Such a conviction is not based on clear thinking. The opposite happens: wherever technology reaches its real fulfillment, it transcends into architecture. It is true that architecture depends on facts, but its real field of activity is the realm of significance."

As Fitch observed, "There is something at once admirable and ornery in his [Mies's] Olympian refusal to lift a finger to help us. . . . To acclaim him for the monumental purity of his form, and yet to deplore his buildings' malfunction in some pragmatic details, is rather like praising the sea for being blue while chiding it for being salty, or admiring the tiger for the beauty of his coat while urging him to become a vegetarian."

Van der Rohe would probably have agreed. Unmoved by the Farnsworth incident, he turned right around and designed two more all-glass buildings without interior support—a drive-in restaurant in Indianapolis, Indiana, and the Fifty-by-Fifty-Foot House, called "the most radical of Mies's efforts over the past thirty years to simplify, articulate and give artistic expression to structural systems."

In 1946 the architect met another idealist like himself and took to him at once. This was twenty-nine-year-old Herbert Greenwald, a former philosophy student who had somehow become a real estate investor and builder. The two talked philosophy together by the hour. Before long they were planning the Promontory Apartments for an area of Chicago near Lake Michigan.

This was just after the war, and a number of projects patterned after design concepts and building methods from the 1920s had failed because of high construction costs. Chicago newspapers broadcast the demise of the high-rise structure and forecast that all future urban residential buildings would consist of garden apartments limited to seven stories. No wonder Mies's Promontory plan was turned down by every mortgage broker Greenwald approached.

"It looks like a Boston sugar warehouse," said one. "How can people live with so much glass?" asked another. "There's no privacy."

Eventually a daring cosmopolitan was won over, however, and the reinforced-concrete structure rose on Lake Shore Drive. (Two preliminary steel versions had been rejected.) Bays were filled in with brick and glass. The facade was subtly elongated by Mies's device of making columns progressively smaller as they approached the roof line. A glass-enclosed recessed lobby formed an effective and appropriately simple entrance at the ground level.

This building, in which van der Rohe's simplicity and logic were combined with Greenwald's practical utopianism, proved that architects could continue building skyscrapers economically and well. Extending the skin-and-bones requirements from architecture to engineering resulted in better concrete control, radiant heating, a modern electrical distribution system—all of which set new standards of excellence for housing. The principles developed in the Promontory construction were later used by the Chicago Housing Authority in several thousand housing units.

And they were used again by Mies and Greenwald in 1950 on another Lake Michigan site, where two side-by-side steel and glass towers went up majestically against the sky. Rising twenty-six stories high, these twin crystal shafts stood on a travertine platform lifted two stories off the ground by steel columns. A black steel canopy joined the buildings at ground level. Vertical beams of black steel projected, at intervals, from the glass facade (a departure from the flat surfaces of Mies's earlier work).

The general concept of the apartment houses' design—free-standing skyscrapers of glass and steel and brilliant architectural detail—revolutionized high-rise planning. They were called van der Rohe's strongest work, his first American masterpiece. Interior photos appeared in *Life* magazine. Around the world the structures at 860 Lake Shore Drive became known simply as "Mies 860."

The openness of the apartments made them extremely flexible; tenants could decorate and furnish them to their own liking. But all renters had to accept the gray fiberglass curtains Mies specified for every floor-to-ceiling window.

Soon there were the usual complaints of excessive heat, intolerable glare, high operating costs, and lack of privacy. But a lively little old lady said she finally had the front porch she'd always wanted. And composer John Cage, admiring a sudden flash of lightning through his all-glass walls, remarked to a visitor, "Wasn't it clever of Mies to make the lightning?" Such pleased tenants kept the 860 vacancy and turnover rate substantially below average.

Mies was never one of his own building's tenants, even though a unit was reserved for him, and Greenwald and others urged him to move in.

In many ways this most modern builder was very old-fashioned. A pocket timepiece always hung from a gold chain across his waistcoat, and he preferred to remain in his high-ceilinged, old-fashioned apartment. There he could have anonymity, whereas at 860, fellow tenants might badger him. Another factor was his slow-motion nature, his distaste for dislocation or travel of any kind. So even though only a block or two separated Mies's old rooms from his beautiful new building, he stayed put.

In the early stages of the Twin Towers project, it was important to convince backer Robert Hall McCormick that the buildings would be a credit to him and his family. The architect devoted much time to developing a precise model and mounting it on his office table at proper viewing height. Then Mr. McCormick was brought in one evening in his wheelchair to see the model. After a few anxious moments, the gentleman was heard to say, "It is a fit monument for any man."

So successful was this "monument" that two aluminum and glass towers joined the originals farther up along Chicago's north shore. And Greenwald was developing practical but less distinguished versions in Detroit, Brooklyn, Manhattan's Battery Park, and Newark. And later there were to be others in Baltimore, San Mateo, Canada, even as far away as London. Soon Mies was spending a major portion of time on urban development projects financed by his friend Greenwald. As one observer has noted, "Mies's technological classicism was eminently reproducible, and it covered the land with modular glass curtain walls from sea to shining sea."

At the same time he was also working on more IIT campus structures, serving a term as president of the International

Congress of Modern Architecture, and compiling, with Philip Johnson, an extensive monograph to accompany an exhibit of his work by the Museum of Modern Art. Though this exhibit shocked conservatives, it won plaudits in such publications as the *Architectural Record.*

He also designed a multipurpose convention hall for Chicago at the request of the South Side Planning Board. Although it was never built, he always named it among his six favorite works. It was a monumental building designed to accommodate fifty thousand people. Its roof would have spanned seven hundred and twenty feet, roughly two city blocks, without any interior columns at all.

In 1958, the year Mies retired from teaching, he began his magnum opus—his first Manhattan skyscraper. The thirty-eight-story headquarters of the house of Seagram was the first bronze-sheathed high-rise ever built. Often called the country's most handsome and impressive office building, it was designed by Mies in collaboration with Johnson. Here, forty years after his 1919 origin of the species, the architect showed definitively what a skyscraper could be. And he reached the point with fewer than ten tall designs, more than half of them unexecuted projects.

Set back one hundred feet from the sidewalk, the building was fronted by a tranquil plaza with trees, greenery, pools, siding of green marble and granite, and a fountain, the model of which was tested in a laboratory at the Massachusetts Institute of Technology. The plaza served as a pedestal from which the tower soared upward five hundred and twenty feet. The exterior bronze lent a warmth that critics had often accused Mies of lacking. ("Some people say that what I do is cold," the architect said once. "That is ridiculous. You can say a glass of milk is warm or cold, but not architecture.") The bronze surface was to be hand-wiped from top to bottom with lemon whenever it got blotchy, van der Rohe stipulated.

Seldom has a building been designed so painstakingly throughout. The architect studied the outer edge of his proposed H-shaped mullions to see how they would relate to the whole twenty-eight-foot-high vertical scale. When he decided to add an eighth of an inch to each of the thousands of mullions, it added thousands of dollars to the proposed thirty-million-dollar cost. Mies was unintimidated. One friend remarked, "He insisted on simplicity, no matter what the cost." Another cracked, "I have never seen more of less."

Mies's insistence that a four-inch module be used throughout the building consigned craftsmen to weeks of redesigning door handles, mail chutes and even fire alarms. A glass manufacturer turned out subtly tinted topaz glass to cut down the glare of the sun. The aluminum industry developed a lighter, more waterproof cover for skeletal steel and unusually long and strong beams of aluminum specifically for the Seagram building.

The interior, largely credited to Johnson, contained all the rich materials Mies's buildings were noted for: elevator lobbies had travertine walls and palazzo floors; office walls were covered with vinyl plastic; the executive men's room was a little retreat of travertine, white leather, stainless steel, and glass.

As the architect had ordained, every day, as darkness fell, recessed ceiling lights automatically went on at a uniform intensity so that the Seagram tower was a giant, glowing shaft punctuating Manhattan's skyline.

There were difficulties along the way. One was cost. Per square foot, the Seagram building was probably the most expensive skyscraper ever built up to that time. Also, an entirely different building had been originally planned by architects hired by Seagram president Samuel Bronfman. That one might have gone up if Bronfman's daughter, then living in Europe, hadn't happened to glimpse a magazine picture of the proposed structure. It looked like a design for a gift decanter, she thought, and flew back to help choose another plan and builder—the best that money could buy. She chose Mies after countless interviews and consultations.

Then there were some anxious moments when it was discovered that Chicago's Mies did not have a license to practice in New York, did not have the high school diploma required for a license anyway, and refused to take the prescribed examination to get one.

Eventually, though, all the red tape was snipped, mainly

through the efforts of Mies's friend Philip Johnson. The building formally opened in the summer of 1958. Mies said proudly, "This is my strongest work." British architect Peter Smithson remarked, "Everything else in Manhattan now looks like a junked-up supermart." Architect Gordon Bunshaft commented, "That old Dutcher expresses steel and America better than anyone." Well satisfied with her choice, Bronfman's daughter summed up the general reaction: "You feel its force and restfulness. Love has gone into it—love for every detail."

Almost every noted New York architect attended the Seagram dedication. But Mies himself was not there. His legs were almost completely paralyzed from recurring attacks of arthritis. In the following year, 1959, he was to receive another painful blow. About to board a plane in Santiago, where he was to start work on the Bacardi Company's glass and concrete office building, Mies spotted a newspaper headline. A plane had crashed into New York's East River. "That's incredible," the architect remarked to the assistant accompanying him. "How can anyone crash into that little stream?" Later, back in Manhattan, Mies found out that his friend Herb Greenwald, forty-two, had been among those killed in the crash.

Van der Rohe tried to bury his grief by throwing himself into projects he and Greenwald had planned, and into solo ones.

The Bacardi office building in Santiago was never built, but the plans constituted a significant development in clear-span designing. A coffered roof seemed to float almost twenty-five feet above the paved pedestal on which the structure rested. To preserve the vast, open quality of the main glass room, Mies deposited most of the divisions and services in a basement. (He did the same thing at ITT's Crown Hall, allowing architectural students to use the huge main room for drafting and relegating the design students to spaces in a semibasement below.)

While Bacardi's Santiago structure remained on the drawing board, the company commissioned the architect to build an office building for them in Mexico City. And this did go up. In 1959 the seventy-three-year-old Mies was very busy indeed. He worked on his first European commission in thirty years—a design for the Friedrich Krupp administration building in Essen, Germany. And on the new Consulate General building in Sao Paulo, Brazil, at the request of the United States State Department. There was also Lafayette Park, a housing project in Detroit, his first mixture of high and low buildings; and then there were the three buildings of the Chicago Federal Center. These three—courthouse, office building, and post office—were perfect examples of ultimate simplicity and studied proportion, so different from the massive domes and porticoes historically used in such civic monuments.

And in 1959 his new Cullinan Wing for the Houston Museum of Fine Arts was opened. Mies attended in a wheelchair.

Long-deserved awards and honors were also finally coming his way. In the summer of 1959 he journeyed to London to receive the Royal Gold Medal for Architecture from Queen Elizabeth II. In his native Germany, he was awarded an honorary doctorate and an order of merit. (A few years later he received the Institute of German Architects' Gold Medal.) In 1960, while in San Francisco to accept AIA recognition, he expressed gratitude for having had the opportunity to teach and work in the United States. The government reciprocated three years later by making him the country's first architect to get the coveted Presidential Medal of Freedom, the highest recognition for a civilian.

Museums all over the world displayed his models and designs. Everywhere he traveled, crowds pressed for a glimpse of this inscrutable person. As for the still shy architect, he always returned from such trips to the seclusion of his Chicago apartment with a sigh of relief.

One of the octogenarian's last journeys was to witness the roof-hoisting operation for a new national gallery he built near the Berlin Wall in the late 1960s. As the 1250-ton crown of prefabricated steel was lifted hydraulically twenty-eight feet up in a mere eight hours and fifty-seven minutes, someone asked Mies how it all looked to him. "Enormous," he replied, grinning and puffing on his cigar.

At the dedication a year and a half later, museum directors also seemed overwhelmed by the huge structure. "A wonderful design for a railroad shed," pronounced one. Others complained that lighting in the downstairs galleries cast shadows on the walls, and that the upstairs hall dwarfed most of the day's art. Similar comments were heard in 1973 at the dedication of Mies's Brown Wing at the Houston Museum of Fine Arts—stiff lighting; elevators too small to accommodate large-scale paintings; and no walls to hang paintings on. (Three walls were of glass and a third side was an open-interval balcony, so curators had to lug in movable screens for the paintings.)

"Apart from the Houston Astrodome," snapped one critic, "one could hardly imagine a less sympathetic space for showing art." Yet the vast curving hall, longer than a football field and twenty-two feet high, was also termed "a jewel of sober, lucid design, its every junction a perfect example of the architect's meticulousness." And Peter Blake said of van der Rohe's Berlin gallery, "What Mies has done here, with this huge hall of glass and steel, seems almost unfair; without intending to do so, he has made most twentieth-century architecture look nearly amateurish. This was built with so incredible a degree of professionalism that one must go to disciplines other than architecture to find its match."

Mies was not present at the dedication of either the Berlin or the Houston museum hall. At the time of the dedication in Berlin he was ill; he remained in Chicago at his doctor's orders. The Houston project was completed after his death by a staff who refused to deviate one iota from the master's plan. But if he had been there and heard the criticisms (no experts complain more about their quarters than museum directors, it is said), it is easy to imagine what Mies would have said.

Asked in a 1965 interview, "Do you design for yourself or for your client?" he replied, "I build not for myself, not for my client. I build for the sake of architecture." And to the interviewer's next query, "Do you consider all designs more important than the needs of people using your buildings?" the architect answered, "I think personal needs are taken care of in all my buildings, but not personal whims."

In his lifetime Mies produced a complete "pattern book" of details, proportions, and forms that could be used by anyone.

And unlike most modernists, who were angered by imitation, he deliberately made them easy to copy. "I have tried to make an architecture for a technological society," he said in 1966. "I have wanted to make everything reasonable and clear—to have an architecture that anyone can build."

When Mies saw many clumsy and inept duplications of his style spring up across the globe, he was not angry—he felt that this was inevitable. "Certainly it is not necessary or possible to invent a new architecture every morning," he declared. Architects would continue to copy, he felt, but with greater discipline. "And you will shortly see the difference in the finished buildings between the greater and lesser talents."

Mies's great talent was that within one structural system, sheathed with the same enclosures of metal and glass, he was able to serve the most varied and unrelated architectural needs. Consider the diverse projects on which he was working or serving as consultant at the time of his death: a classroom building for Drake University, apartment buildings for Baltimore and Detroit, a downtown development complex for Montreal, a library for Washington, D.C., a science center for Duquesne University, a service station, a broadcasting studio, a housing project for London, and his final skyscraper, the IBM building in Chicago.

On August 17, 1969, at the age of eighty-three, the architect died in Chicago's Wesley Memorial Hospital, two weeks after admittance. Modest to the end, he said in one of his last interviews that he never regretted any of his structures not being built. Each had been the object of his own interest and had not been conceived out of a desire to win a competition or to win fame.

As for what he felt influenced his architectural development the most, Mies said, "I thought a lot and I controlled my thoughts in my work—and I controlled my work through my thoughts. . . . I had no conventional architectural education. I worked under a few good architects, I read a few good books, and that's about it."

In an age of complexity and confusion, Mies was a purist. In an age of innovation, he was a disciplinarian. He never swerved from the path he'd set upon in youth. This singleness of purpose is evident in the sixty years' worth of architectural drawings that he willed to the New York Museum of Modern Art.

"In over half a century of architectural practice," said James Marston Fitch, "Mies van der Rohe has displayed an imperturbable, almost glacial continuity in his work. . . . This unchanging and unchangeable path appears in retrospect both heroic and endearing. It establishes the fact that he is incorruptible, absolutely impervious to the dictates of fad and fashion, to the club and carrot techniques which society employs to bring balky artists to heel."

Because the architect always wanted not to change the time but to express the time, he would probably smile with pleasure at the tribute *New York Times* writer Ada Louise Huxtable paid him after his death: "The glassy skyscraper and sleek-walled buildings that are the pride of modern cities and the symbol of modern life owe more to Mies van der Rohe than to any other architect of our time. . . . What he did, essentially, was to give that age its characteristic look and style. . . . The reduction of much large-scale utilitarian building to simple, practical 'Miesian' elements has resulted in a valid and handsome, genuinely vernacular architecture for our day."

Walter Gropius

Unity in Diversity

An Early Success

There is an old shoe factory in northern Germany that is a national monument. If you drove by it today, unaware of its genesis, you probably wouldn't give it a second glance. Constructed of steel frame and masonry with metal and glass walls, it's a kind of building that's now fairly commonplace.

But in its time—1911—it was a stunning architectural achievement, hailed as the first truly modern factory. And what is even more impressive, it was the first independent project carried out by its designer, then just twenty-eight years old.

The architect was Walter Gropius, and the Fagus shoe factory was the first milestone in a brilliant career. Gropius would later emerge as one of the prime shapers of modern architecture and the most influential force in architectural education.

Even the usually silent Mies van der Rohe rose to his feet at a luncheon in Chicago in the 1950s on the occasion of Gropius's seventieth birthday. He paid tribute to his colleague's work, then referred to the Fagus project, saying: "This building was so excellent that he became, with one stroke, one of the leading architects in the world."

The commission for the now-famous shoe factory, the kind of opportunity young architects dream about, did not come easily to Gropius. In those days, he was working, along with Le Corbusier and Mies van der Rohe, in the Berlin offices of Peter Behrens, a noted German architect. Eager to get out on his own, he began a letter-writing campaign. In his spare time he pored over newspapers and other periodicals, searching for notices of expansion and other indications of possible new building projects. Every time he spotted such a lead, he fired off a letter offering his services. Hundreds of such letters flowed from his pen; hundreds of rejections flowed back to him.

On December 7, 1910, young Gropius wrote just such a letter to German industrialist Carl Benscheidt, who, he had learned, was planning a new factory in the small community of Alfeld. Gropius cited his training and his experience in the office of the well-known Behrens. He concluded that he would carry out the project "in a way both artistic and practical."

Benscheidt, struck by the letter from the unknown architect, invited Gropius to submit his design. Immediately impressed by it—even though it was radical for its day—Benscheidt persuaded his board of directors to approve it.

The Fagus factory, with its simple lines and lightness, is a hybrid of concrete, brick and steel. Suspended on the outside are daringly cantilevered corner beams and non-load-bearing curtain walls of glass and metal. The columns are moved back from their traditional corner position, and the corners are formed by the glass screens.

The young architect's curtain walls showed clearly that the walls no longer supported and carried the structure, a function carried out by the skeleton steel frame. As Gropius himself said: "The role of the walls become restricted to that of mere screens stretched between the upright columns of the framework to keep out rain, cold, and noise."

In those days of heavy-set structures with massive corner columns, and styles harking back to previous centuries, the Fagus factory was a significant departure. It was a structure of its time, carried out with the materials and technology of its time. And as such it reached a new height in grace and buoyancy.

As architectural authority Sigfried Giedion said, Gropius had "discovered the art form of the steel-framed structure, and in the process had presented a new architectural vocabulary."

Walter Adolf Gropius was born May 18, 1883. High interest and distinguished participation in art, architecture, and the crafts were a family tradition; Walter's ancestors were noted for the very kind of innovation and experimentation with new materials that were to mark Walter's career.

One of his forebears, Carl Gropius, a businessman and a painter, was a figure in the art world of Berlin in the early years of the nineteenth century. He was known for a large diorama (a transparent three-dimensional picture) that he completed in 1827. Martin Gropius, Walter's great-uncle, was an architect and educator; he had designed the Museum of Arts and Crafts in Berlin in the mid-nineteenth century. He later served as principal of the city's arts and crafts school and achieved a reputation for advancing its standards of design. Walter's father, after whom he was named, was a surveyor for the city of Berlin; he was also a painter and was active in art publications.

As a boy, Walter lived with his father and his mother, Manon Gropius, in an apartment in Berlin. But two of his mother's uncles had rural estates in Pomerania and Posen, and the Gropius family retreated to the country whenever possible. It was on one of these estates, his uncle Erich's in Pomerania, that Walter first had a hand in design and construction. While still a student, he helped plan and build several workmen's houses.

Young Gropius studied architecture at the University of Charlottenburg, Berlin, and then at the University of Munich. His education was interrupted in 1904 by a year of compulsory military service, and then again in 1907, when he inherited some money from an aunt and decided to travel.

He went to England, Italy, and then Spain. He toured important buildings, studied in ceramics, and worked in a pottery factory. After a year he returned to Berlin. Largely because of his brilliant record as a student, he landed an apprenticeship to architect Behrens. Although he was limited at first to designing lighting fixtures, his talent for originality showed almost immediately. Soon he was the famous architect's chief assistant, taking part in design projects ranging from individual products to factories and office buildings.

Gropius found his work in the Behrens office challenging, and he enjoyed the companionship of his colleagues. Among the architect's fondest memories were those of his twenty-seventh birthday, when Le Corbusier, Mies van der Rohe, and other co-workers threw a party for him. It was a modest affair in the back room of a cheap Berlin restaurant, but Gropius said it was one of the happiest evenings he ever spent.

Gropius, however, was determined to forge his own independent career, so he embarked on the solicitation campaign that led to the Fagus factory assignment.

The architectural success of the shoe factory led to other commissions. Gropius, now in his own office and assisted by fellow architect Adolph Meyer, had the opportunity to show his extraordinary versatility. He designed residences, wood furniture for a luxurious villa, steel furniture for a battleship, a sleeping car for the German railways, and a diesel locomotive for a railway factory in Koenigsberg. In 1913 he submitted some of his designs to a world exhibition in Ghent, Belgium, and was awarded a gold medal. Another exhibition the next year in Cologne provided the springboard for a project that was to become the second important milestone of his career.

Gropius was an active member of the German Werkbund, an organization of artists, craftsmen, and representatives of industry. Their goal was to improve the design and production of the goods and facilities of industry.

For its 1914 Cologne exhibition, the Werkbund constructed a wide variety of creative designs for industry. The assignment given to Gropius: a model factory.

Because funds were so limited, it was not an easy task. Gropius traveled throughout Germany soliciting a contribution from one company, bricks from another company, promises of building materials from others. Despite these problems, the industrial complex he designed for the Werkbund exhibition was the most exciting architectural event of the show.

The complex had three major elements: an administration building, a garage compound, and a medium-sized factory. The administrative section, which drew the most attention at the exhibition, had spiral concrete stairs at each end. The stairs were cantilevered out from a central column and enclosed in a cylindrical glass curtain wall. The effect was stunning: the stairway, stripped of its usual enclosure, seemed to float in space, a new height in the use of transparency in architecture. As one critic said, the achievement brought poetry to the industrial process and seemed even to celebrate the efficiency of the machine.

Gropius was a sensation at a very early age. Then his career was interrupted: World War I broke out, and Gropius, an officer in the cavalry, was called immediately to service.

House of Building

Gropius served his country with distinction, and when he returned to civilian life in 1918 he wore the first-class and the second-class Iron Cross, the Bavarian Military Medal, and the Royal Austrian Decoration. He survived the crash when his observation plane was shot down; after one conflict he lay wounded for hours under a layer of corpses before medical aides found him. Away from the front, he devised a new signaling system that the German army adopted.

While he was in a forward hospital being treated for wounds, Gropius received a letter from Alma Mahler, a woman he'd met several years before while vacationing in Switzerland. She was the young widow of the celebrated German composer Gustav Mahler, and she wrote to congratulate him on his work at the Cologne exhibition.

Gropius answered her letter, and they began corresponding regularly. In 1915, while he was on a two-week leave in Berlin, they met and fell in love. Later that year they were married, although they could be together only when he managed a rare brief leave from his military unit. In 1916 Alma wrote him that she had borne his child, a girl whom they named Manon after his mother.

During one of his leaves, something occurred that would significantly alter the course of his professional life. The grand duke of Weimar summoned him for an interview and asked him if he would, at war's end, take on direction of the School of Arts and Crafts there.

Gropius hesitated. He would be following in the footsteps of Henry van Velde, the eminent Belgian architect. And although Weimar was a small community, it had been the home of the noted German author Goethe and had a long tradition as a center of culture. Unable to resist the challenge, Gropius accepted the offer.

The architect returned to the world of peace with mixed emotions. On the one hand was the exciting prospect of his new post. He had given a great deal of thought to design education during the war years and was anxious to put his ideas to work. And his confidence had grown when he had learned that it was van Velde himself who had recommended him as "the only man in Germany" who could do the job.

At the same time, Gropius learned from his wife Alma that, during his absence, she had fallen in love with the German poet Franz Werfel. This was a crushing blow to Gropius. At his urging, Alma agreed to make an effort to preserve their marriage. But it failed, and they were divorced.

Gropius directed all his energies toward his work, and in no way did he minimize the task before him.

"I had found my own ground in architecture before the war," he later wrote about this point in his life. "The full consciousness of my responsibility as an architect, based on my own reflection, came to me as a result of the war—during which my theoretical premises first took shape. . . .

"It was then that the immensity of the mission of the architect of my own generation first dawned on me. I saw that, first of all, a new scope for architecture had to be outlined, which I could not hope to realize alone, but which would have to be achieved by training and preparing a new generation of architects. . . ."

That was the goal Gropius set for himself. And beneath that goal were certain principles that would underlie his own work and that of the teachers and students who came under his influence during this important stage of his career.

Gropius had long believed in the union of art and industry. The machine, he was convinced, was the modern medium of design, and designers had to come to terms with it. The academies where young artists and sculptors studied had lost touch with the real world; they had isolated the artist from his environment. Art for art's sake was obsolete.

He believed in the union of arts and crafts, of head and hand, of theory and practice, of intellectual and manual work. Not only was there a common citizenship bonding all creative work; the arts and crafts were all dependent on one another.

While keenly aware of the difference between competence and high creativity, he believed that every artist was first of all a craftsman, and that arbitrary divisions between the two had to be broken down for the enhancement of both.

Above all, he believed in collaboration, in teamwork based on the notion that the problems of creating designs for man's environment were larger than any one man or any one discipline. In an age of specialists, he was a universalist. And it was in this respect that Gropius most differed from Wright, Le Corbusier, and even Mies van der Rohe. Although they, like Gropius, were in the forefront of the architectural revolution then in its early years, each was a highly individualistic artist whose achievements rested largely on supremely creative personal talents. To Gropius, brilliant designer though he was, architecture was "supra-personal"—reaching out beyond the periphery of the talent of any individual. His goal, to be sure, was to lead, but to lead a team, to serve as a catalyst, bringing together diverse capabilities for achievement of a higher order. It was a principle that would remain with Gropius throughout his long career, both in the United States and abroad.

Upon tackling his new assignment in early 1919, Gropius's first move was a characteristic one: he merged the Weimar Academy of Fine Arts with the School of Arts and Crafts. He gave the new entity a new name—Bauhaus, or House of Building. It was a name that would achieve a singular stature in the world of design.

Gropius knew that to realize his goal for the school, he would need a staff of collaborators and assistants who would, as he said, "work not as an orchestra obeying the conductor's baton, but independently, although in close cooperation to further a common cause." He was firm in the belief that the art of building, the supreme art embracing all others, was contingent upon the coordinated teamwork of a bank of active collaborators.

For his staff, Gropius recruited some of the most talented, progressive artists and craftsmen in Europe. They were also some of the most controversial. They were identified with the often-abused "modern movement," and were hardly the favorites of the establishment of the day.

"It was sheer madness," wrote historian Sigfried Giedion, "to jeopardize one's reputation and position by the appointment of such artists as government servants in a state institution . . . artists whose significance was appreciated only by a very small circle and whose work had excited the strongest expressions of outrage, abuse and detestation throughout Germany and even beyond its borders. But with this group of derided outcasts, Walter Gropius then proceeded . . ."

Gropius put together a four-page publication for prospective students of the Bauhaus, and in it he outlined the philosophy behind the new undertaking: "The final product of all artistic endeavors is the building. The visual arts once found their highest task in contributing to beauty and were inseparable constituents of all great works of architecture. Today each stands apart in independent isolation, and the situation can only be changed through conscious cooperative work. Architects, painters, sculptors must again come together and study the many-sided nature of the building, both as a whole and in all its several parts. Only then will their work again express the spirit of great architecture and be freed from the dead hand of academicism."

Response was immediate. Students, intrigued by the new

master and his new ideas, came from all over the country. Some young artists arrived with only the shabby clothes they wore and the examples of their work that they carried. These specimens Gropius judged carefully, as they were the major clues to the student's aptitude. But it was an inefficient selection process at best, Gropius realized, and he rarely denied young artists at least a trial period.

Young men turned up still wearing the remains of their army uniforms; young women left their jobs in arts and crafts shops and their classes in academies to make their way to Weimar. One young man, an apprentice house painter, told later how he had literally dropped his brush when he saw the Gropius leaflet and headed for the school.

Gropius knew he had quite a chore before him: on the one hand, a faculty made up of artists whose work made cultural traditionalists uneasy, to say the least; on the other hand, a group of students of all descriptions, not unlike later bands of beatniks or hippies.

Most important, Gropius knew that the whole scheme of his educational experiment was a ticklish one—combining imaginative design and technical proficiency. But he was convinced that man's only chance to avoid enslavement by the machine was through achieving mastery of it. The Bauhaus would be more than a school—it would be a bridge between art and technology.

As the program took shape, it became evident that Gropius was a master organizer, a born teacher. Never interested in turning out small replicas of himself, he gave his faculty and his students wide freedom for individual expression—within the realm of the school's goals. At the same time he believed in general rudimentary training. All students went through the same basic course of study, regardless of their individual ambitions. Then they were permitted to specialize.

The basic six-month course was designed to introduce the student to proportion and scale, rhythm, light, shade, and colors, and to give him experience with materials and tools of all kinds, including those of industry. The student was exposed to all the essentials of design, including the scientific principles of optics and optical illusion, and to the techniques and materials he would need to carry out ideas.

After this preliminary training, the student entered one of the workshops for an intensive three-year period of productive learning. There were workshops in ceramics, carpentry, metalwork, weaving, painting, sculpture, furniture design, stained glass, and, later, typography and stage design.

In the workshop the student learned under two masters— one a handicraft master, the other a master of design. "The idea of starting with two different groups of teachers was a necessity," Gropius recalled later, "because neither artists possessing sufficient technical knowledge nor craftsmen with sufficient imagination for artistic problems were to be found. A new generation capable of combining both these attributes had first to be trained. In later years, the Bauhaus succeeded in placing as masters in charge of workshops former students who were then equipped with such equivalent technical and artistic experience."

At the end of his three workshop years, the Bauhaus student underwent examination by his faculty members and by the local Chamber of Handicrafts. Those who passed were awarded a journeyman's certificate. At that point, if he or she so desired and was judged capable, the student went on to the third phase of the Bauhaus program, the culmination of all previous work—the building training. Here, he studied architectural design, draftsmanship, and engineering. Again, the theoretical was merged with the practical: the student worked not only in the classroom but also at actual building sites, taking part in practical experiments with new building materials and new design solutions. For this training he received the master certificate of the Bauhaus. He was then equipped for a career as architect or teacher, whichever was his bent.

In operation, the learning experience at the Bauhaus was much less rigid than the course descriptions suggested. It was a laboratory, a place where new ideas were constantly emerging, being tested, and then being abandoned or adopted. Chance was the order of the day, and the moment a better solution was discovered, it was taken up. Faculty members and students alike were charged individuals, dedicated to being part of a movement they believed was creating a new order of art. Disagreements were not uncommon. Some of the artists took to wearing odd clothes and carved wooden shoes and shaving their heads. Gropius finally insisted on reasonably conventional dress, reminding them that artists must accept their time—and the dress that goes with it.

Occasionally, selected Bauhaus students were sent out to do practical work in factories as part of their training, and sometimes skilled workmen came from factories into Bauhaus workshops to discuss the needs of industry with teachers and students. Gropius solicited commercial commissions from industry to design products; some manufacturers signed contracts with the school, and later royalty payments helped pay bills.

Funding was a constant problem in the first years of the Bauhaus in Weimar. The design work being done there represented a radical departure from tradition. Conservatives in the area, unaccustomed to designs based on the geometric forms of modern art rather than on earlier historic styles, reacted against the school, its teachers and its students. They charged that the Bauhaus people were all socialists, and local government leaders, sensitive to public opinion, made it increasingly difficult for Gropius to get the money he needed to run the state-supported school.

To counteract mounting feeling against himself, his staff, and his students, Gropius scheduled open houses at the Bauhaus, where he exhibited student products and had staff members deliver lectures. Some new friends were won, but the undercurrent of friction remained.

In 1923 Gropius and his associates held a "Bauhaus Week," a festival-exhibition to show the world the fruits of the first four years of the new school. The work of teachers and students in virtually every art and craft was put on display: abstract paintings, woven fabrics, pieces of sculpture, chinaware, varied teapots made from identical components, lamps, chairs and other furniture designed for machine production, and an experimental building.

The designs were functional, clean of line, stripped of ornamentation; they owed nothing to historic styles. In short, they were modern in every sense (and would still be modern today). "I was astonished by all that I saw," wrote one critic. He went on to praise the group for its "unswerving pursuit of its objectives in spite of the present situation in Germany, which makes her the slave of immediate necessity; in spite of paltry funds; in spite of cheap ridicule; in spite of malicious attacks from reactionaries; and, not least, in spite of internal difficulties. These objectives are to discover the new principles of form which are essential if the creative forces of the individual are to be reconciled with industrial production."

That same year, 1923, Gropius went to Hannover, Germany, to deliver a lecture. While there he met a young woman named Ise Frank. Her beauty and intelligence, along with her intense interest in his work, impressed Gropius, and they were soon married. From then on Ise was at his side, working to solve problems at the Bauhaus.

And problems at the school mounted. Ridicule and repeated charges that Gropius, a lifelong democrat, was the leader of a band of socialists didn't bother him as much as the problem of getting the funds to run the school, a task which became more and more difficult. In 1925, Gropius called his faculty members and students together and sadly announced that the school would close.

But the Bauhaus had made its mark, and when news of its plight got out, four cities contacted Gropius, all offering financial support for an expanded Bauhaus if he would locate it within their boundaries.

Impressed by the natural setting and by the enthusiastic support of city officials there, Gropius chose Dessau, a town about an hour's drive from Berlin. In the spring of 1925, Bauhaus masters and students packed up and moved to the new location to pursue their work.

The move not only put the school on firm financial footing for the first time, but gave Gropius the opportunity to extend the range and mastery of his own architectural prowess by designing the new structures to house the school. The result was another Gropius master stroke.

In his Bauhaus complex, Gropius carried out his maxim that buildings should be "not monuments but receptacles for the flow of life they have to serve." The main Bauhaus building, made of reinforced concrete and brick, had glass curtain walls that were even more striking than those of Gropius's Fagus factory. The free-standing walls were connected to cantilevered floor edges, and columns were set back from the paned glass, giving the entire structure a light, airy quality.

A taller student residence with exterior balconies held individual combination living-studio rooms. There was also a workshop wing. Connecting these elements were bridgelike structures on piers—one held a student canteen, auditorium and stage; the other contained administrative offices. There were separate duplexes for faculty members. For himself and Ise, there was a house in the woods a few hundred yards from the main complex. Flat roofs, liberal use of glass, exterior balconies, and unadorned geometric form characterized all the structures.

The entire Bauhaus building complex is looked upon today as a classic of the adolescent years of modern architecture.

The Bauhaus prospered in its new location for a time. Students completed their training and went on to serve industry or architecture or education—or themselves. New students arrived, anxiously seeking entry. Departments were expanded, programs added. It was becoming an institution, a force in the world of design.

For Gropius, this meant that he had a little more time to devote to his own design career. He designed a municipal employment office for Dessau, a low-lying semicircular structure with a rectangular wing; a housing unit in nearby Toerten, with homes ingeniously assembled from standardized prefabricated parts; and a "total theatre," with a revolving stage that could be repositioned within a structure, designed to eliminate any division between actor and spectator. The theatre design attracted a great deal of attention in professional circles but, for economic reasons, was never constructed.

Characteristically, Gropius involved his best students in his own projects. Also characteristically, he continued to devote the majority of his energy to the continuing development of the school. But economic and political forces combined to hamper his efforts.

Germany's economic condition was going from bad to worse. At the same time, a political entity called the Nazi party, led by one Adolf Hitler, was rising to power. The radical designers of the Bauhaus were even more heatedly accused of radicalism in politics. They were branded Bolshevists, degenerates, communists. Political activists mounted campaigns, calling upon the Dessau citizenry to protest the very presence of the school in their area. Financial support from the local government became harder and harder to get.

Some of the criticism was aimed at Gropius personally, and he finally decided that the Bauhaus and the principles it represented might stand a better chance of surviving without him.

In February 1928 Gropius submitted his resignation to city authorities. He didn't tell his students immediately, because a social affair had been planned for that evening and he didn't want to put a damper on the party. Late that night, however, word reached the Bauhaus that posters announcing Gropius's resignation had appeared in town.

A band that had been playing stopped its music. A senior student approached Gropius. "There is no one to fill your shoes, Gropius," he said, touching the master's arm. "You ought not to leave us." Moved and embarrassed, Gropius walked to the center of the room and tried to explain to his students why he was leaving. Before he could finish, students had closed in on him and lifted him to their shoulders in tribute.

Gropius's old colleague, Mies van der Rohe, later took over direction of the school, but its future was short. As the result of mounting pressure and harassment from Hitler's Nazi party, he soon closed the Bauhaus down.

Although short-lived as educational institutions go, the Bauhaus kindled and flamed a revolution in the teaching of painting, sculpture, industrial arts, and architecture. And its influence reached out through the Western world.

Gropius's educational experiment was, in every sense, a success. As he said later: "I felt [at the time of his departure from Dessau] that the intellectual objective of the Bauhaus had been fully achieved."

Architect in Exile

Gropius and Ise returned to Berlin, where Gropius threw himself into his private practice. Versatility was his hallmark. He designed everything from shops to stoves. For an automobile company, he designed a convertible coupe with two seats that reclined, bedlike.

Especially interested in housing—and the structural and social challenges therein—he became a member of the board of experts of the Reichs Research Institute for Economic Building and Housing. He designed two housing projects near Berlin which won the institute's first prize; he experimented with prefabricated houses made of copper plate; and he built the first slablike multistory apartment dwellings in Germany.

With his usual thoroughness, he did time and motion studies of labor-saving devices in both construction and use of houses, explored various industrialized approaches, and experimented with on-site assembly of components made elsewhere. Gropius strove for individual touches even in his row houses. To avoid the wall-like appearance of many row houses, and to give equal access to sunlight, he angled each unit.

And, as usual, Gropius thought in larger terms: "My idea of the architect as the coordinator—whose business is to unify the various formal, technical and economic problems that arise in connection with building—inevitably led me on, step by step, from study of the function of the house to that of the street; from the street to the town; and finally to the still vaster implications of regional and national planning."

In 1930 the German Werkbund was asked to take part in a new exhibition in Paris, and the organization's leaders turned immediately to Gropius. Would he be their commissioner and take complete responsibility for the exhibit? Gropius enthusiastically agreed to put together the display for the Paris exhibit and called upon several of his former colleagues from the Bauhaus to work with him on the project.

In 1929 Gropius had written a paper for an international architectural conference on the social bases of various kinds of dwellings. In it, he talked of single-story buildings, walk-ups, and high-rise structures, and went to great lengths to analyze problems of land coverage and to examine the importance of psychological and social values.

He recognized the need for privacy in the urban community—he advocated a room of his own, however small, for every grown-up person. But he also recognized that communality had to be given shape and heart: "The essential provision of a large, communal scale for community facilities such as playgrounds, community kitchens, play spaces, nursery schools, shops, mechanical equipment must not only be assured, but the building of the community center must come first before any houses are built or any dwellings are built."

For the German Werkbund's exhibition at the Paris show, Gropius and his colleagues designed precisely that: the community center of a ten-story apartment house. And it was one of the most successful displays of the entire exhibition.

As people approached the Werkbund section of the Paris show, the first thing they saw was the glass walls of a swimming pool and a gymnasium. One writer said at the time that it was a typical Gropius subtlety, "opening the exhibit with an overture." Beyond the swimming area was a leisure area with a bar,

Mies van der Rohe, 1958. *Courtesy, Wide World Photos*

Drawing, the Kroller House, The Hague, Holland, 1912. *Courtesy, Museum of Modern Art, New York*

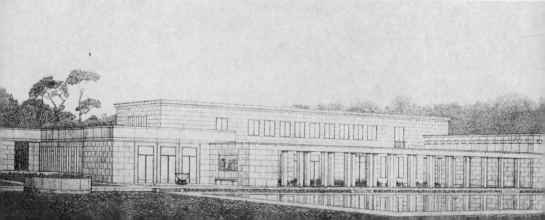

Interior living area, Tugendhat House, Brno, Czechoslovakia, 1930.
Courtesy, Museum of Modern Art, New York

German Pavilion, International Exposition, Barcelona, Spain, 1939.
Courtesy, Museum of Modern Art, New York.

Apartment houses, Lake Shore Drive, Chicago, Illinois, 1951. *Courtesy, Fujikawa Conterato Lohan and Associates*

Seagram Building, New York, 1958. *Courtesy, Joseph E. Seagram and Sons*

One IBM Plaza, Chicago, Illinois, 1970. *Courtesy,
Fujikawa Conterato Lohan and Associates*

Mies van der Rohe, with model of the School of Architecture and
Design, Illinois Institute of Technology, 1952. *Courtesy, Wide World
Photos*

The Fagus Factory, Alfeld, Germany, 1911. *Courtesy, Museum of Modern Art, New York*

Walter Gropius at Harvard University in the 1950s. In the background, the Harvard Graduate Center. *Courtesy, Harvard News Office*

(ABOVE) United States Embassy, Athens, Greece, 1954. *Courtesy, U.S. Department of State.* (BELOW) Side view. *Courtesy, The Architects Collaborative*

(OPPOSITE, TOP) The Bauhaus Building, Dessau, Germany, 1925. *Courtesy, Museum of Modern Art, New York*

(CENTER) The Gropius House, Lincoln, Massachusetts, 1938. *Courtesy, Museum of Modern Art, New York*

(BOTTOM) Harvard Graduate Center, Cambridge, Massachusetts, 1949. *Courtesy, Harvard News Office*

The Thomas Glass Factory, Amberg, Germany, 1968. *Courtesy, The Architects Collaborative*

Walter Gropius in later years. *Courtesy, New York* Times

a dance floor, reading and playing corners, a library, and a radio-phonograph nook. A metal bridge of open latticelike steel rose over the swimming pool.

A wide variety of lighting effects was achieved by skillful use of standardized lighting fixtures, from reading lamps to large illuminations. There was a display of woolen fabrics stretched over square frames that seemed to hover in space. Mass-produced chairs designed by Bauhaus masters stood out at right angles from the wall, all the way up to the ceiling. And there was a model apartment with a general living area, bathroom, kitchen, man's study, lady's boudoir, and workroom (office). Among its appointments: revolving standardized cupboards, chairs of tubular steel, and movable writing desks.

The structure, the furniture, the fixtures—all were in essence as simple and functional and modern as anything we see today, nearly half a century later. In addition there was, again, that quality of lightness. As one Parisian critic wrote: "The first and most striking feature of the German exhibit is lightness. This exhibit has one most important aspect which none can escape and which we require to study very carefully. . . ."

There was more to the exhibit, for it suggested not only a new way of designing and a new way of building and planning, but also a new way of living.

The German ambassador in Paris, who had been very nervous about the "radical" nature of the planned display, was surprised and delighted by the cordial reception given to the show by the people and the press. He held a formal reception for Gropius and his fellow artists at the palatial embassy, inviting leading French architects and artists to meet them.

Gropius's reputation was, by this time, assured and growing. He was awarded an honorary doctoral degree by the Hannover Institute of Technology, and was elected vice-president of the International Congress of Modern Architecture. But still he found himself in an alien political environment.

The first years of the 1930s, during which Gropius was engaged in private practice in Berlin, were the years when Hitler and the Nazi party, which had been gaining strength since the 1920s, rose to full power. Although he loved his native Germany, Gropius was opposed to everything the new regime represented. In 1933 Gropius and Ise decided they had to leave their country.

It wasn't that simple. Although Hitler didn't look with favor on the modern movement in art and architecture, or its leaders, he didn't want native talent leaving the country.

It was an invitation to speak at an international theatre conference in Rome that gave Gropius and Ise their chance. They attended the meeting, where he delivered a lecture on the architect and the theatre. Then he, Ise, and their adopted daughter Beate went directly to London, where they took up residence in exile.

Gropius went into practice with E. Maxwell Fry, a modern English architect whose work had impressed him. They collaborated on several houses and then on a building complex for Impington Village College in Cambridge. A low, sprawling structure, this building was designed for use by both children and adults. A two-story assembly hall with a stage served as an auditorium for children during the day and as a meeting place for adults in the evening. Adjoining this were a dining room with kitchen, a common room, rooms for table tennis and billiards, a library, small lecture rooms, and a workshop with a blacksmith forge. From the assembly hall a promenade passed two administrative staff offices and led to the wing of individual one-story classrooms and science laboratories which had walls that were virtually all glass. This classroom arrangement has since been widely adopted in Europe and in the United States.

While in England, where he had more time for design and for thought, Gropius wrote a book, *The New Architecture and the Bauhaus.* In it he outlined not only the goals and methods of the Bauhaus, but the principles and nature of the new modern architecture then emerging.

"A breach has been made with the past which allows us to envisage a new aspect of architecture corresponding to the technical civilization of the age we live in," he wrote. "The morphology of dead styles has been destroyed, and we are returning to honesty of thought and feeling. . . .

"The liberation of architecture from the welter of ornament, the emphasis on its structural functions, and the concentration on concise and economical solutions represent the purely material side of the formulizing process on which the practical value of the new architecture depends. The other, the aesthetic satisfaction of the human soul, is just as important as the material. Both find their counterpart in the unity which is life itself. What is far more important than the structural economy and its functional emphasis is the intellectual achievement which has made possible a new spatial vision. For whereas building is merely a matter of methods and materials, architecture implies the mastery of space."

Gropius went on to discuss the new materials, steel, concrete, and glass; the skeletal frame which had relieved walls of their traditional support function, thus opening them to bolder treatment and new kinds of windows; and the advantages of flat roofs.

"The new architecture," he wrote, "throws open its walls like curtains to admit a plenitude of fresh air, daylight and sunshine. Instead of anchoring buildings ponderously into the ground with massive foundations, it poises them lightly, yet firmly, upon the face of the earth and bodies itself forth not in stylistic imitation or ornamental frippery, but in those simple and sharply modeled designs in which every part merges naturally into the comprehensive volume of the whole. . . . The ethical necessity of the new architecture can no longer be called in doubt."

Gropius had thought when he left Germany that he would be returning in a few years. But as the political situation in Germany deteriorated, it became increasingly clear to him that he might never return. In 1937 James B. Conant, president of Harvard University, met with Gropius in England. He explained that the university wanted to bring new ideas to its architectural education program and offered Gropius a post as senior professor.

Gropius, always the teacher, accepted. Before he left, a group headed by the eminent author H. G. Wells sponsored a farewell dinner for the architect. The spirit of the occasion was captured when writer Herbert Read offered the toast: "Gropius belongs to the world."

Shortly after arriving in the United States, Gropius was asked to address a group of architects. It was an important occasion for him for several reasons. Principal among them was the matter of styles and labels. Although he derived great satisfaction from his achievements with the Bauhaus and with his own practice, he strongly opposed the labels attached to this work— "Bauhaus style," "international style," "functional style." While addressing this subject, he made clear the essence of his theories about architectural education: "My intention is not to introduce a, so to speak, modern style from Europe, but rather to introduce a method of approach which allows one to tackle a problem according to its peculiar conditions.

"I want a young architect to be able to find his way in whatever circumstances; I want him independently to create true, genuine forms out of the technical, economic, and social conditions in which he finds himself, instead of imposing a learned formula onto surroundings which may call for an entirely different solution. It is not so much a ready-made dogma that I want to teach, but an attitude toward the problems of our generation which is unbiased, original and elastic.

"It would be an absolute horror for me if my appointment would result in the multiplication of a fixed idea of 'Gropius architecture.' What I do want is to make young people realize how inexhaustible the means of creation are if they make use of the innumerable modern products of our age, and to encourage these young people in finding their own solutions . . .

"My ideas have often been interpreted as the peak of rationalization and mechanization. This gives quite a wrong picture of my endeavors. I have always emphasized that the other aspect, the satisfaction of the human soul, is just as important as the achievement of the material, and that the achievement of a new spatial vision means more than structural economy and functional perfection. The slogan 'fitness for purpose equals beauty' is only half true. When do we call a human face beautiful? Every face is fit for purpose in its parts, but only perfect proportions and colors in a well-balanced harmony deserve that title of honor 'beautiful.' Just the same is true in architecture. Only perfect harmony in its technical functions as well as in its proportions can result in beauty. That makes our task so manifold and complex."

In less than a year, Gropius was appointed chairman of the Department of Architecture of Harvard's Graduate School of Design. He would hold the position for fifteen years, and in those years Harvard would become known as one of the major forces in architectural education in the world.

A few of his colleagues from the Bauhaus joined Gropius on the Harvard faculty, but he made no attempt to bring his Bauhaus curriculum to the school—it would not have been appropriate. He did, however, apply his basic principle: integrating architecture, town planning, and landscape architecture. And he strove for closer contact with other disciplines, such as those of the social sciences and the humanities. He continued to stress the maximum development of the individual within the realm of collaboration with specialists from other fields, all geared to a larger overall goal.

He stressed attitudes and methods over information—the search over research. He related the role of the architect to the realm of citizenry, and positioned architecture within democracy, stressing the responsibilities of the individual and the profession.

A former student once wrote: "Gropius was the first man who interpreted the industrial revolution to us in terms of architecture, in terms of design, in terms of community planning. He constantly investigated the great potentialities of industrial society and showed us how to assimilate them to our ever-changing needs.

"Looking back, we who have been Gropius's students can say gratefully that he has shown us a place in society; that he has taught that mechanization and individual freedom are not incompatible; that he has explained to us the possibilities and values of communal action, and I shall always doubt that a lesser human being could have given us that new faith in the world."

Gropius's idea that the architect must find his way within the peculiar circumstances of any given project was never better exemplified than in the design of his own house in Massachusetts.

Shortly after arriving at Harvard, Gropius chose a site in Lincoln, about a half-hour drive from the university. It was on the crest of a hill in the middle of an apple orchard, not far from the Walden Pond made famous by writer Henry Thoreau.

At first glance, the Gropius house appeared to be a typical contemporary piece of the period: flat roof, extensive use of glass, simple geometric lines. Closer examination showed that it acknowledged New England traditions and blended with them. It was a wood-frame structure sheathed with white clapboard siding, materials very much at home in the area. But the siding ran vertically instead of horizontally. The idea of the porch, also a traditional element, struck Gropius. But instead of making his porch part of the basic house structure itself, he projected it out from the house into space. For their teenage daughter Beate, Gropius created a private entrance in the form of a steel spiral stairway leading to her second-floor bedroom. A large window wall stretching from the dining room to the living room provided a broad view of the woods and hills. At the front of the house, a canopy, partly protected by a glass wall, projected out at an angle. And jutting into the rear garden was a wooden trellis for climbing plants.

Some years later Gropius recalled the project in a speech to architectural students in Chicago: "Building near Walden Pond in the New England countryside, we became the neighbors of John Adams, one of the direct descendants of the president, and we were rather worried over what we thought might have been a very sour reaction from a family so steeped in history. But old Mr. Adams took one good look, and to our surprise he said he thought this modern house was actually more in keeping with the New England tradition of simplicity than quite a few other solutions that had been tried. He was a little disturbed by the unfamiliar sight of the flat roof and other unconventional characteristics. . . . [But] he could see that the moving spirit behind it was facing a problem in much the same way in which the early builders of the region had faced it when, with the best technical means at their disposal, they built unostentatious, clearly defined buildings that were able to withstand the rigors of the climate and that expressed the social attitude of the inhabitants."

One critic wrote that, as with so many Gropius buildings, there was an "inherent rightness" about his house that became increasingly apparent with passing time.

In association with Marcel Breuer, who collaborated with him on a number or projects, including his own house, Gropius did several more houses in New England and, in 1941, a series of row houses in New Kensington, Pennsylvania, for workers at an aluminum factory.

But, although he was aware of and somewhat dismayed by the fact that American society tended to look upon teachers as less than doers, Gropius's main efforts in these years were directed toward broadening and sharpening the educational experience of his students. In addition to widening the range of the course of study and closing gaps between architecture and other disciplines, he insisted that each student spend six months on an actual construction project. One must, he said, work with materials firsthand, and wrestle firsthand with pragmatic on-the-spot building problems. It was an extension of his workshop theory at the Bauhaus.

Gropius's position grew increasingly firm within academic as well as professional architectural circles. He was made an honorary Phi Beta Kappa, and was awarded an honorary master's degree by Harvard. He was elected to membership in the American Society of Planners and Architects, and he became a fellow of the American Academy of Arts and Sciences. Western Reserve University bestowed on him an honorary doctoral degree, and he was made an honorary fellow of architectural groups in England, Mexico, and France.

At the insistence of his wife Ise, Gropius edited his various writings for a book: *Scope of Total Architecture.* In it he advanced his theories on planning, housing, the education of architects, and the place of the architect in society. In his preface for the volume he wrote:

"Since my early youth I have been acutely aware of the

chaotic ugliness of our modern man-made environment when compared to the unity and beauty of old, pre-industrial towns. In the course of my life I became more and more convinced that the usual practice of architects to relieve the dominating disjointed pattern here and there by a beautiful building is most inadequate and that we must find, instead, a new set of values, based on such constituent factors as would generate an integrated expression of the thought and feeling of our time."

This is the essence of the social commitment that Gropius felt very strongly and that fathered the dedication to teaching which he exhibited throughout most of his adult life. At the same time, he was ever driven to pursue his goals for architecture through his practice.

Shortly after World War II, while still heading the Harvard School of Architecture, Gropius went into a practicing partnership with seven younger architects, several of whom were former students. Typically, he named the firm The Architects Collaborative (TAC). The agreement was that all would be equals, but one member would be "captain" for each project they undertook. The move opened a new chapter in the life of Walter Gropius the architect.

"My reputation has penetrated . . ."

In 1952, at age sixty-nine, Gropius retired from his post at Harvard. He had no intention of "sitting around under the trees," as he phrased it; instead he began what proved to be the busiest time of his life in terms of sheer architectural production.

One reporter chronicled the start of Gropius's "retirement" day this way: "At about 8:10 A.M. the old gent dashes from his house in Lincoln, Massachusetts, often clutching a brown paper bag with one banana and one Swiss cheese on rye, no mustard. He takes the wheel of his golden Rambler and drives very fast through snarled Boston traffic to arrive at the Cambridge office of The Architects Collaborative at 8:55, five minutes before anyone else gets there. He has a compulsion to be first."

An early project of the Collaborative was the Harvard Graduate Center, a complex of seven dormitories (to house five hundred and seventy-five students) and a commons, or student center. The dormitory buildings, linked by covered passageways, are two-story and three-story structures built of reinforced concrete and glass, with buff brick facing: a sharp contrast to the red brick masonry of the traditional Harvard buildings. The upper walls of the commons, the only curved structure of the complex, are mainly of glass.

A notable feature of the commons is the integration of contemporary art: a brick mural by one artist . . . a glazed tile design by another . . . a large wall painting by still another. The basic idea is that the works of contemporary artists should be daily companions of student life.

The design for the Harvard Center was awarded a Gold Medal by the Architectural League of New York. Other school commissions came to the Collaborative, notably one for a junior high school in Attleboro, Massachusetts. This building, constructed on varied levels to accommodate an uneven site, has been described as "symbolizing unconstrained American youth."

Gropius and his colleagues were busier than ever. They designed houses, schools, a housing development in Lexington, Massachusetts, a larger housing project in West Berlin, and the twenty-five-million-dollar John F. Kennedy federal office building in Boston. The latter structure is divided into two parts—a twenty-six-story double tower and a four-story low building—and flexibility in office space is achieved by modular planning based on a square grid with four-foot-ten-inch sides.

Then, in 1959, came an unusually important assignment—a

new United States Embassy building for Athens, Greece, a mile from the Parthenon.

The task was a tricky one. It was to be a showcase of modern American architecture, but at the same time it had to be compatible with its classic surroundings. It was to create a warm, friendly, inviting atmosphere, expressive of American democracy. Needless to say, many people who thought of Gropius as one of the high priests of functional, unadorned modern architecture were not optimistic about the outcome.

Gropius and his associates at the Collaborative went to work, and the resulting design was spectacular: decidedly Greek in feeling; elegant, yet modern in design. The most pessimistic observers were surprised and delighted.

The striking embassy building is a three-story structure of reinforced concrete, and around it are tall columns, visible girders, and horizontal ribbons—all sheathed in the shining white Pentellic marble used in the Parthenon itself. The structural arrangement gives the building a light, hovering effect. The design forms a twenty-foot cantilever, reminiscent of ancient Greek porticoes, which shields the two upper floors from the intense glare of the Greek sky. A screen of sky-blue ceramic tile rings the first floor; around the upper two floors is a gray glass curtain wall. Like the houses of ancient Greece, the building is constructed around an interior court ringed with columns.

"We did our best to connect the city's traditions with our own architectural concepts," Gropius said. "But keeping the traditional does not mean to imitate."

The embassy was called a triumph of architectural diplomacy; a subtle blending of the elegant and the approachable, the traditional and the contemporary; authoritative, yet friendly.

New honors came to Gropius from around the world. The Far East Society of Architecture awarded him its Silver Medal of Achievement. The University of Sydney, Australia, the University of Brazil, and other institutions gave him new honorary degrees. In 1959, while the embassy in Athens was being built, the American Institute of Architects honored him with its Gold Medal. Britain's Royal Society of Arts presented him with its Prince Albert Gold Medal.

"My reputation has penetrated through," Gropius commented about this time in his career. "Now these things come to me." He served as design consultant for the Pan American building in New York, a fifty-nine-story commercial structure overlooking Park Avenue from its footing in the area of Grand Central Station. And for the government of Iraq, Gropius and his Collaborative colleagues designed an entire campus of buildings to accommodate the twelve thousand students of the University of Baghdad. It was a huge, seventy-million-dollar project, with clusters of air-conditioned buildings set close together to provide shade in one-hundred-twenty-degree summer heat. Concrete shells covered the combined theatre, auditorium, and mosque. Water from the nearby Tigris River splashed in garden courts.

There was a new fineness, a new elegance reflected in the structures Gropius designed in his later years. He himself observed: "I was possibly too Puritan—too much storming against the old traditions. Now I have with the same conceptions, I hope, a more subtle, more delicate expression." And, although he was one of the key people in freeing architecture from the bonds of history, Gropius expressed concern over a lack of discipline. "When I arrived in the United States it was still possible in Massachusetts to squelch an unusual proposal with the words 'it isn't done.' No such code exists today; everything can be done and most certainly is being done. Our cities have taken on the look of the free-for-all. All sense of propriety and discrimination seems to have been swept away by this unlimited technical dam-burst. The whole population must develop a sense of beauty, a sense of the eye."

In 1963 Gropius, then in his eightieth year, delivered an address at Williams College. It was apparent that his basic beliefs and his faith in education had not changed over the long years since he had been at the Bauhaus.

Technology has thrown man out of balance, Gropius told his audience, and has overshadowed other components which are indispensable to the harmony of life. Yet in the last resort, he said, mechanization must have only one purpose: to reduce the individual's physical toil in order that hand and brain may be set free for a higher order of activity.

"Our problem is to find the right balance and coordination between the artist, the scientist, and businessman," he added, "for only together can they create humanized standard products and build with them a harmonious entity of our physical surrounding."

Gropius urged that technology be counterweighted by increased emphasis on education in the arts and humanities, and, returning to his favorite theme, he called for an exalted spirit of collaboration. "As a successful democracy hinges on our ability to cooperate," he said, "we need the technique of collaboration in teams. The essence of such techniques should be to emphasize individual freedom of initiative instead of authoritative direction by a boss. Synchronizing all individual efforts by a continuous give-and-take of its members, the team can raise its integrated work to higher potentials than the sum of work of just so many individuals."

In the summer of 1969, following complications after heart surgery, Gropius died in a Boston hospital at the age of eighty-six. There was no funeral in the customary sense. Instead, following instructions he had written many years before, some seventy friends gathered in the wood-paneled conference room of The Architects Collaborative offices in Cambridge, shared a drink, and reminisced about the master. "Wear no sign of mourning," he had written. "It would be beautiful if my friends would get together—drinking, laughing, loving—all more fruitful than graveyard oratory."

He was totally active until his final illness, and at his death the Collaborative had some three hundred million dollars' worth of work in progress, including a satellite city outside Berlin, a vast medical complex in Boston, and a World Trade Center in Teheran.

Newsweek described Gropius as "one of the brilliant fathers of modern architecture." *Time* called him "modern architecture's idea-giver." Eminent architect Richard J. Neutra wrote that he was "a wizard of precious human metallurgy."

But most moving, and most applicable to Gropius himself, were the words he wrote a few years before death to a group of high school students who had asked career advice:

"For whatever profession, your inner devotion to the tasks you have set yourself must be so deep that you can never be deflected from your aim. However often the thread may be torn out of your hands, you must develop enough patience to wind it up again and again.

"Act as if you were going to live forever and cast your plans way ahead. By this I mean that you must feel responsible without time limitation, and the consideration whether you may be around to see the results should never enter your thoughts.

"If your contribution has been vital there will always be somebody to pick up where you left off. And that will be your claim to immortality."

Acknowledgments

The authors owe a large debt of gratitude to the many architects, architectural scholars, historians, and other commentators included in the bibliography whose books, articles, reports, and other publications were consulted during the preparation of this manuscript.

We are especially indebted to distinguished architect and friend Charles Colbert, who was responsible for first stimulating our interest in architecture many years ago.

Edwin and Joy Hoag
Los Angeles, California
August 1976

192

Bibliography

General

Columbia University School of Architecture. *Four Great Makers of Modern Architecture.* New York: Da Capo Press, 1963.
Forsee, Aylesa. *Men of Modern Architecture.* Philadelphia: Macrae Smith Company, 1966.
Peter, John. *Masters of Modern Architecture.* New York: Bonanza Books, 1958.
Rambert, Charles. *Architecture from Its Origins to the Present Day.* New York: Western Publishing Company, Inc., 1969.
Richards, J. M. *An Introduction to Modern Architects.* Baltimore: Penguin Books, 1940.
Scully, Vincent, Jr. *Modern Architecture.* New York: George Braziller, 1961.

Frank Lloyd Wright

Andrews, Wayne. "The Great Uncompromiser," *Saturday Review,* November 14, 1953. Includes a biographical sketch by B. Kalb.
"Architecture," *The Nation,* April 14, 1962.
"Atomic Mr. Wright," *Newsweek,* May 16, 1955.
Blake, Peter. *Frank Lloyd Wright.* Baltimore: Penguin Books, 1960.
Bush-Brown, Albert. "The Honest Arrogance of Frank Lloyd Wright," *The Atlantic Monthly,* August 1959.
"Cities," *Time,* May 25, 1953.
Farr, Finis. *Frank Lloyd Wright: A Biography.* New York: Charles Scribner's Sons, 1961.
"Finale at Eighty-Nine for a Fiery Genius," *Life,* April 27, 1959.
"FLW: Architecture's Stormy Colossus," *Coronet,* August 1957.
"FL Wright: At Eighty-Four Still Fighting," *Business Week,* October 17, 1953.
Forsee, Aylesa. *Frank Lloyd Wright: Rebel in Concrete.* Philadelphia: Macrae Smith Company, 1959.
"The Great Dissenter," *Newsweek,* April 20, 1959.
"Hero, Prophet, Adventurer," *Saturday Review,* November 7, 1959.

Hoag, Edwin. *American Houses*. Philadelphia: J. B. Lippincott Company, 1964.

House Beautiful. F.L.W., His Contribution to the Beauty of American Life. New York, November 1955.

Jacobs, Herbert. *Frank Lloyd Wright: America's Greatest Architect*. New York: Harcourt, Brace and World, 1965.

Kaufmann, Edgar. *An American Architecture: Frank Lloyd Wright*. New York: Bramhall House, 1955.

Kaufmann, Edgar, and Raeburn, Ben. *Frank Lloyd Wright, Writings and Buildings*. New York: New American Library, 1960.

Kennedy, Robert Woods. "Reconsiderations—The Natural House," *The New Republic*, October 30, 1971.

"Man of Culture: Sixty Years of Living Architecture," *Newsweek*, November 2, 1953.

Marlin, William. "Frank Lloyd Wright: The Enduring Presence," *Saturday Review*, October 4, 1975.

"Native Genius," *Time*, April 20, 1959.

"Naughty Nautilus," *Time*, August 10, 1953.

"Notes and Comments," *New Yorker*, April 18, 1959.

Oboler, Arch. "He's Always Magnificently Wright," *Reader's Digest*, February 1958.

"Portrait," *Time*, June 11, 1969.

"Prairie Skyscraper," *Time*, May 25, 1953.

Scully, Vincent, Jr. *Frank Lloyd Wright*. New York: George Braziller, 1960.

"Titan of Taliesin," *Saturday Review*, December 21, 1957.

Twombly, Robert. *Frank Lloyd Wright*. New York: Harper & Row, 1973.

"What Nature Teaches Man," *Science Digest*, January 1966.

Willard, Charlotte. *Frank Lloyd Wright, American Architect*. New York: Macmillan, 1972.

Wright, Frank Lloyd. *An Autobiography*. New York: Horizon Press, 1943.

Wright, Frank Lloyd. *The Future of Architecture*. New York: Horizon Press, 1953.

Wright, Frank Lloyd. *The Living City*. New York: Horizon Press, 1958.

Wright, Frank Lloyd. *The Natural House*. New York: Horizon Press, 1954.

Wright, Frank Lloyd. *A Testament*. New York: Horizon Press, 1957.

Wright, Olgivanna. *Our House*. New York: Horizon Press, 1959.

Wright, Olgivanna. *The Shining Brow*. New York: Horizon Press, 1960.

"Wright or Wrong," *Time*, March 22, 1954.

"Wright's Might," *Time*, November 9, 1953.

"The Wright Word," *Time*, August 2, 1954.

Le Corbusier

Alazard, Jean. *Le Corbusier*. New York: Universe Books, 1960.

"Architecture," *The Nation*, February 16, 1963.

Besset, Maurice. *Who Was Le Corbusier?* Translated by Robin Kemball. Geneva: Skira, 1968.

Blake, Peter. *Le Corbusier.* Baltimore: Penguin Books, 1960.

"Builder to the Stars," *Senior Scholastic,* November 1958.

"Chapel in Concrete," *Time,* July 18, 1955.

Choay, Francoise. *Le Corbusier.* New York: George Braziller, 1960.

"Corbu," *Time,* May 5, 1961.

Evenson, Norma. *Le Corbusier, The Machine and the Grand Design.* New York: George Braziller, 1969.

"Farewell to Corbu," *Scholastic Arts,* April 1966.

"Future of the City," *Architectural Record,* November 1962.

Gardiner, Stephen. *Le Corbusier.* New York: Viking Press, 1974.

Hauser, Ernest. "Rebel in Concrete," *Saturday Evening Post,* December 8, 1956.

Haverstick, John. "Le Corbusier: The Architect Who Would Synthesize the Arts," *Saturday Review,* August 10, 1957.

Horsley, Carter. "Le Corbusier Vision of a City Rejected in Zoning Plan," *The New York Times,* July 22, 1973.

Jencks, Charles. *Le Corbusier and the Tragic View of Architecture.* Cambridge, Mass.: Harvard University Press, 1973.

Jordan, Robert. *Le Corbusier.* New York: Hill & Company, 1972.

Le Corbusier. *Talk with Students from the Schools of Architecture.* Translated by Pierre Chase. New York: Orion Press, 1961.

"Le Corbusier, A Tribute," *Architectural Forum,* October 1965.

"Le Corbusier, 1887–1965, A Tribute," *Art News,* October 1965.

"Le Corbusier Designs for Harvard," *Architectural Record,* April 1963.

"Le Corbusier's New Masterpiece in Concrete," *Architectural Forum,* September 1962.

"Legacy of a Great Architect," *House and Garden,* February 1968.

"Letter from Paris," *New Yorker,* September 18, 1965.

"Lightning at Chandigarh," *Time,* April 21, 1958.

"The Master Builder," *Newsweek,* September 6, 1965.

"Monks in Concrete," *Time,* June 27, 1960.

Pawley, Martin. *Le Corbusier.* New York: Simon and Schuster, 1971.

"Portrait," *Life,* October 4, 1954.

Rand, Christopher. "Visit to Chandigarh, City on a Tilting Plain," *New Yorker,* April 30, 1955.

"Renaissance on the Riviera," *Saturday Review,* October 24, 1953.

"The Revolutionary," *Time,* September 3, 1965.

"Rites at Louvre for Le Corbusier," *The New York Times,* September 1, 1966.

Scully, Vincent, Jr. "Soaring Legacy of a Titan," *Life,* September 1965.

Serenyi, Peter. *Le Corbusier in Perspective.* New York: Prentice-Hall, 1975.

"Silver, Nathan. "Good-by, Corbusier," *The Nation,* June 17, 1968.

"Skyline: First Maison d'Unité d'Habitation," *New Yorker,* October 5, 1957.

"Stompin' on the Savoye: Villa Savoye," *Time,* March 23, 1959.

Mies van der Rohe

"Architectural Details," *Architectural Record,* October 1963.

"Big Room," *Time,* February 2, 1959.

Blake, Peter. "Mies van der Rohe," *Architectural Forum,* October 1969.

Blaser, V. *Mies van der Rohe.* New York: George Braziller, 1972.

"Continuing Tradition in Great Architecture," *Architectural Forum,* May 1962.

De Long, James. "Mies," *House Beautiful,* November 1969.

Drexler, Arthur. *Mies van der Rohe.* New York: George Braziller, 1960.

Ellwood, Craig. "Mies van der Rohe: Gentle Nonconformist," *The Los Angeles Times,* July 27, 1969.

"Emergence of a Master Architect," *Life,* March 18, 1957.

"Four Architects," *Vogue,* August 1, 1955.

"Glass House Stones: Farnsworth House," *Newsweek,* June 8, 1953.

Hughes, R. "Museum Without Walls," *Time,* October 29, 1973.

Huxtable, Ada Louise. "Soaring Towers Gave Form to an Age," *The New York Times,* August 19, 1969.

"IIT: The House That Mies Built," *Science Digest,* March 19, 1966.

Johnson, Philip. *Mies van der Rohe.* New York: Museum of Modern Art, 1953.

Kuh, Katherine. "Mies van der Rohe: Modern Classicist," *Saturday Review,* January 23, 1965.

"Less Is More," *Time,* June 14, 1954.

McQuade, Walter. "Mies," *Architectural Forum,* October 1969.

"Mies Builds in Mexico, Administration Building for Ron Bacardi Company," *Architectural Forum,* January 1962.

"Mies van der Rohe," *The New York Times,* August 19, 1969.

"Mies van der Rohe: Disciplinarian for a Confused Age," *Time,* August 29, 1969.

"Monument in Bronze," *Time,* March 3, 1958.

"New Work of Mies van der Rohe," *Architectural Forum,* September 1963.

"Obituary," *Architectural Record,* September 1969.

Shirley, David. "Mies the Master," *Newsweek,* September 1, 1969.

"Skyline, the Lesson of the Master," *New Yorker,* September 13, 1958.

Speyer, James. *Mies van der Rohe.* Chicago: Art Institute of Chicago, 1968.

Stern, Richard. "Mies and the Closing of the Bauhaus," *The Nation,* September 22, 1969.

"Westmount Square," *Architectural Forum,* August 1969.

Walter Gropius

Abercrombie, Stanley. "Bauhaus Birthday: Art, Architecture, Revolution," *The Wall Street Journal,* October 16, 1969.

Andrews, Wayne. "Harvard's Old Master," *Saturday Review,* March 26, 1955.

"Architectural Genius Gropius Dies," *Sunday Herald Traveler,* July 6, 1969.

"Architecture for Athena," *Time,* July 15, 1957.

"Art and Industry," *New Republic,* December 13, 1954.

"Bauhaus," *Publishers Weekly,* September 1, 1969.

"Bauhaus Builder," *Time,* June 1, 1953.

Blake, Peter. "All Purpose Old Master of Design," *Life,* June 7, 1968.

"Curse of Conformity," *Saturday Evening Post,* September 6, 1958.

"Custom Wall Progression in the Work of Walter Gropius," *Architectural Record,* February 1965.

"Dedicated Materialists?" *Newsweek,* January 15, 1962.

"Everybody's Baby," *Time,* July 14, 1961.

Fitch, James. *Walter Gropius.* New York: George Braziller, 1960.

Franciscono, M. "Walter Gropius and the Creation of the Bauhaus in Wiemar," Review in the *Architectural Forum,* January 1972.

"German Pioneers of Modern Design," *Life,* November 25, 1957.

Giedion, Sigfried. *Walter Gropius: Work and Teamwork.* New York: Reinhold, 1954.

Gropius, Walter. *The New Architecture and the Bauhaus.* New York: Museum of Modern Art, 1956.

Gropius, Walter. *Scope of Total Architecture.* New York: Macmillan, 1955.

"Gropius, the Shaper of Modern Design, Dies in Boston at 86," *The New York Times,* July 5, 1969.

"Gropius Addresses Convocation at Williams," *Architectural Record,* November 1963.

"Gropius' 80th Birthday Marked by Old Friends and Students," *Architectural Record,* July 1963.

"The Idea-Giver," *Time,* July 18, 1969.

"John Fitzgerald Kennedy Federal Office Building, Boston," *Architectural Record,* February 1965.

"Last Word of Gropius," *Architectural Record,* August 1969.

"The Lawgiver," *Time,* June 29, 1959.

"Neutra Pays Tribute to Walter Gropius," *The Los Angeles Times,* July 7, 1969.

"New Tribute to Walter Gropius," *Architectural Record,* May 1968.

Reinhold, Robert. "Mark Architect's Death," *The New York Times,* July 7, 1969.

Shirley, David. "Testament of Joy," *Newsweek,* July 21, 1969.

"Symbol, Sculpture for Pan Am Building, New York," *New Yorker,* April 8, 1961.

"United States Embassy, Athens, Greece," *Architectural Record,* February 1961.

Von Eckardt, Wolf. "Gropius: Young at His Passing," *The Washington Post,* July 31, 1969.

"Walter Gropius, Work and Teamwork," Review in *New Yorker,* December 18, 1954.

Glossary

Aggregate: Sand or gravel or other material which, when added to cement and water, makes concrete.

Arcade: A long arched building or arched covered passageway.

Ashlar: A facing made of squared stones or thin slabs used to cover walls of brick or rubble.

Avant-garde: Person or group that develops new or experimental concepts, especially in the arts.

Byzantine: In the manner of the style of architecture of the Byzantine Empire of the fifth and sixth centuries.

Canopy: Ornamental rooflike structure projecting from a building as a shelter from adverse weather.

Cantilever: A beam or girder or other structural member whose unsupported projection is counterbalanced by weight or other support at the opposite end.

Casement: A window sash that opens on hinges on the side; a window with such a sash.

Clapboard: A narrow board, usually thicker at one edge than the other, used for siding and applied horizontally and overlapping.

Column and slab construction: A method of building which utilizes an upright member (column) and, as a base, any stratified or flat oblong surface (slab).

Cornice: The molded and projecting top horizontal member of a structure; often a decorative band of metal or wood.

Curtain wall: A thin wall that supports no weight, often positioned in front of the principal structure of steel or concrete.

Curvilinear: Consisting of or bounded by curved lines.

Cyclopean legs: Columns of gigantic masonry which give an impression of resistance and power.

Dormer: A window set vertically into a structure and projecting through a sloping roof.

Façade: The front of a building, or any other exterior side given special architectural treatment.

Folded roof: Ribbed covering that assumes the form of pleats or folds.

Free façade: Exterior walls of a building that are not loadbearing and can be opened up or closed at will.

Functionalism: The philosophy of design which holds that form should be adapted to use, material, and structure; that the prime design consideration should be the purpose of a building.

Gable: A vertical triangular portion of the end of a building, from cornices or eaves to ridge.

Girder: A horizontal main structural member that supports vertical loads.

Gothic: The style of architecture of medieval Europe, twelfth to sixteenth centuries.

Greek Revival: The period in the first half of the nineteenth century when architects and builders copied the styles of the temples of ancient Greece.

Inglenook: A wide recessed fireplace arrangement or chimney opening, usually flanked by bench-type seats.

Internationalist: Follower of the International Style or International School, the dominant architectural current in the second quarter of the twentieth century.

Loadbearing wall: A wall that helps support the ceiling, floor or roof above it.

Lozenge: A figure with four equal sides and two acute and two obtuse angles.

Modernist: One who upholds the value of new techniques and teachings as opposed to classical ones.

Modular: Constructed with standardized units or dimensions for flexibility and variety in use.

Modulor: A scale of proportions laid down by Le Corbusier and his colleagues and related to the proportions of the human body.

Mullion: A slender vertical member of a structure placed between windows or doors or used decoratively on a building's surface.

Non-loadbearing wall: A wall which carries no weight above it but is used merely to divide space.

Open plan: An architectural design or structural system employing a very few widely spaced columns that permit the utmost freedom in the arrangement of partitions and other space divisions.

Organic architecture: Architecture, principally associated with Frank Lloyd Wright, in which great emphasis is placed on harmony of structure and site.

Parapet: A low wall or railing designed to protect the edge of a roof or platform; often merely ornamental.

Pavilion: A partially enclosed structure, usually roofed, in a garden, park or place of recreation or entertainment, often light and ornamental.

Penthouse: A structure or dwelling built on the roof of a building.

Piazza: A porch or veranda; an open square in a European town.

Pier: A pillar that supports an arch; pillars or columns designed to support the weight of the structural members above.

Pilotis: A series of piles holding up a building and liberating the space beneath.

Plywood: Structural material made of thin sheets of wood glued or cemented together, with the grains of adjacent layers at right angles to one another.

Poured concrete: A building material composed of water, cement, and an aggregate, which may be gravel, sand, crushed stone, or a combination, applied in a semi-liquid state.

Prairie houses: Houses of a style originated by Frank Lloyd Wright: simple structures with low-slung roof planes, wide projecting eaves, and earth-hugging, emphatic horizontal lines.

Prefabrication: A method of construction in which component parts of a structure, such as wall or window sections, are manufactured for assembly later at the building site.

Promenade: A place for strolling.

Queen Anne style: The style of architecture associated with the reign of Queen Anne, 1702–1714; an elegant, picturesque and spectacular style.

Rafter: Any of the often sloping, evenly spaced parallel beams that support a roof.

Refectory: The dining hall of a monastery.

Reinforced concrete: Concrete strengthened by iron or steel rods within it.

Rendering: In architecture, a drawing or other artistic representation of a structure.

Retaining wall: A wall, usually of concrete with heavy iron or steel reinforcement, constructed to hold back a weight, such as part of a hillside.

Ribbon windows: Windows which round a structure, often including corners, in the manner of a ribbon.

Skylight: An opening in a roof covered with glass or other transparent or translucent material designed to admit light.

Slab: In architecture, the thick layer of concrete that forms the foundation of a structure.

Solarium: A room designed specifically for exposure to the sun.

Split-level: A structure, usually a house, divided vertically so that the floor level of rooms in one part is about midway between the levels of floors in an adjoining part.

Stucco: A material made of cement, sand, and lime and applied wet to form a hard covering for an exterior wall.

Sunbreaker: Recess or projection from the general surface designed to shield the surface from the rays of the sun.

Surrealistic: Having the intense irrational quality of a dream.

Travertine: Mineral found in cave deposits; when solid, banded and responsive to high polish, it is known as Mexican onyx or onyx marble.

Tudor: Architecture of the Tudor period in England, principally the sixteenth century.

Utilitarian: With emphasis on utility, or usefulness, as opposed to appearance.

Utopian: Ideal, visionary; pertaining to Utopia, imaginary place of perfection.

Veneer: A thin sheet of material overlaid on another material for protection or ornamentation.

Victorian: Related to the time and styles of Queen Victoria's reign in England in the late nineteenth century.

Index